# The Duchess
# of Duke Street
# Entertains

# The Cast List for
## *The Duchess of Duke Street*

| | |
|---|---|
| Gemma Jones | Louisa Trotter |
| Christopher Cazenove | Charlie Tyrrell |
| Richard Vernon | Major Smith-Barton |
| John Cater | Starr |
| Victoria Plucknett | Mary |
| Holly De Jong | Violet |
| John Welsh | Merriman |
| Donald Burton | Augustus Trotter |
| George Pravda | Monsieur Alex |
| Bryan Coleman | Lord Henry Norton |
| Sammie Winmill | Ethel |
| Mary Healey | Mrs Cochrane |
| Kate Lansbury | Mrs Wellkin |

# The Duchess of Duke Street Entertains

Edited by Michael Smith

Coward, McCann & Geoghegan, Inc. New York

Books by Michael Smith

*Fine English Cookery*
*Best of British Cookware*
*Kidneys to Caviare*
*Grace and Flavour*

First American Edition 1977

Copyright © 1977 Michael Smith and Egret
Productions Limited

This book is based on the television series *The Duchess
of Duke Street* created and produced by John
Hawkesworth for BBC Television. The author wishes to
thank the BBC and Egret Productions Ltd. for their
co-operation.

All photographs are BBC Copyright.

Line drawings are by Kate Simunek © W. H. Allen
and Co. Ltd., 1977 and those on pages 139, 172 & 204
are by Nicholas Price. © Michael Smith 1977

SBN: 698-10850-7

**Library of Congress Cataloging in Publication Data**
Main entry under title:

The Duchess of Duke Street entertains.

Includes index.
1. Cookery, English. 2. Dinners and dining—
England—London—History. I. Smith, Michael,
1927-    II. The Duchess of Duke Street.
TX717.D78   1977   641.5′941   77-24315

Printed in the United States of America

# Contents

# Acknowledgements

I would like to say a special thank you to the following: to John Hawkesworth for inspiring (and insisting on) an interest for detail in all those who work with him, and of course for thinking the whole thing up.

To Directors Bill Bain, Simon Langton, Cyril Coke and Ray Memuir (who encouraged, looked for, and got near-perfection from the whole team) and their delightful P.A.'s, and to those stalwart Production Assistants who work so tirelessly on the studio floors: Edwina Craze, Ros Parker, Margot Heyhoe and Rosemary Crowson.

The A.F.M.'s — to Rosemary Hesther, Carol Scott, Rosemary Webb and Ann Aronsohn, a very special thank you for teaching me all I now know about life on the studio floors; for their infinite patience, help and — the discipline required of us all in being ready for the cameras.

The P.U.M. — to Marcia Wheeler for stretching her budget — at times when it must have been impossible — so that I could dress the food and dinner tables in a lush manner worthy of Ray Cusick, Paul Joel and Vic Meredith's brilliant sets.

To Ann Ord, Susan Pulbrook, June Wade and Sonja Waites for the exquisite way they interpreted my 'scribbles and sketches' on the 'heavy' table sets.

To Victoria Huxley for being such a helpful editor.

To Pat Brayne (the only person *ever* to interpret my handwriting successfully), for the speed and accuracy with which she has typed my manuscripts.

And to my family and friends, and anybody I have missed, for their encouraging support and practical help seeing to my laundry, dusting, shopping, car-ferrying, et al. And, last but by no means least, to my canine pal 'Chippo' for waiting — some days up to eighteen hours — before he got taken out for his pee!

# Concerning Tables

It is virtually impossible to give exact equivalents of British/American/Metric measures in a book of this nature, as the conversion ratio changes quite radically after the initial 'common denominator' has been established, and which common denominator differs with each ingredient: liquid, avoirdupois and volume. It would appear on the face of things that butter, margarine, cooking fats would all be the same, but this is not so.

Therefore the following tables are purely guidelines — and approximate at that — and the cook must use his or her knowledge of local habits and ingredients to arrive at a satisfactory result (levelling up or down where it appears appropriate, and relating to personal well-tried recipes).

The important differences are between firstly the *British* (20 fluid ounces) and the *American* (16 fluid ounces) *pint*. Adjusting the liquid content of a recipe is the most essential factor (and perhaps the easiest to do); and secondly the *volume* between 'whipped' cooking fats and 'solid' ones varies considerably from brand to brand. Only trial and error will establish matters here once and for all.

# Metric

1 British ounce equals 28.31 grammes — taken to 4 decimal places. Rounded down to 28 grammes per ounce creates a table as follows:

28 grms   1 oz.

56 grms   2 ozs.

112 grms   4 ozs.

225 grms   8 ozs.

450 grms   1 lb.

Remembering that a metric pound (livre) is counted as 500 grammes or half a kilo(gramme)!

# Liquid Measurements

## British

1 pint (20 fluid ounces)

$\frac{1}{2}$ pint (10 fluid ounces)

$\frac{1}{4}$ pint (5 fluid ounces)

## American

1 pint (16 fluid ounces)

$\frac{1}{2}$ pint (8 fluid ounces)

$\frac{1}{4}$ pint (4 fluid ounces)

## British/Metric

35 fluid ounces ($1\frac{3}{4}$ British pints)         = 1 litre

$17\frac{1}{2}$ fluid ounces (a 'good' $\frac{3}{4}$ British pint) = $\frac{1}{2}$ litre

$8\frac{3}{4}$ fluid ounces (a 'scant' British $\frac{1}{2}$ pint) = $\frac{1}{4}$ litre

1 British (Imperial) pint         = 575 millilitres
                                     (i.e. equals a
                                     'good' half litre)
                                     1 litre equalling
                                     1000 ml.

# Approximate equivalent measures of the major foodstuffs

|  | *British* | *American* | *Metric* |
|---|---|---|---|
| Breadcrumbs (white, dry) | | | |
| Butter (margarine — not the whipped variety — lard, etc.) | 1 lb. (16 ozs.) | 2 cups | 450 grms (metric pound is 500 grms, or a 'scant' British 1¼ lbs.) |
| | ½ lb. (8 ozs.) | 1 cup | 225 grms |
| | ¼ lb. (4 ozs.) | ½ cup | 112 grms |
| | 2 ozs. | ¼ cup | 56 grms |
| Cheese, grated | 1 lb. | 4 cups | 450 grms |
| Chocolate | 1 oz. | 1 square | 30 grms |
| Cornflour (Cornstarch) | 4½ ozs. | 1 cup | 128 grms |
| Currants, Raisins, Sultanas etc. (the larger the berry the greater the volume in cups) | 1 lb. | 2½ cups | 450 grms |

| Flour(s) | 1 lb. | 4 generous cups | 450 grms |
| | 4 ozs. | 1 generous cup | 112 grms |
| | 2 ozs. | ½ cup | 56 grms |
| Sugar | 1 lb. | 2 generous cups | 450 grms |

# Oven Temperatures

| °F | °C | Gas Mark No. | |
|---|---|---|---|
| 250 | 130 | ½ | Very cool |
| 275 | 140 | 1 | Still very cool |
| 300 | 150 | 2 | Slow |
| 350 | 180 | 4 | Moderate |
| 400 | 200 | 6 | Hot |
| 425/450 | 220/230 | 7/8 | Hot/very hot |
| 500 | 260 | 9 | 'Roasting' hot |

# Ingredients

| English | American |
|---------|----------|
| Aubergine | Eggplant |
| Bacon rashers | Bacon slices |
| Bicarbonate of Soda | Baking Soda |
| Biscuits | Crackers or Cookies |
| Biscuit mixture | Cookie dough |
| Boiling chicken | Stewing chicken |
| Broad beans | Fava or Lima beans |
| Cake mixture | Cake batter |
| Celery stick | Celery stalk |
| Chicken/Beef stock cube | Bouillon cube |
| Chicory | Belgian endive |
| Cocoa powder | Unsweetened cocoa |
| Cooking apple | Baking apple |
| Cooking chocolate | Unsweetened cooking chocolate |
| Cornflour | Cornstarch |

| English | American |
|---|---|
| Courgettes | Small zucchini |
| Crystallised fruits | Candied fruits |
| Crystallised ginger | Candied ginger |
| Demerara sugar | Light brown sugar |
| Digestive biscuits | Graham crackers |
| Double cream | Whipping cream |
| Essence | Extract |
| Fine breadcrumbs | Fine dry breadcrumbs |
| Fresh beetroot | Raw beets |
| Fresh vegetables | Raw vegetables |
| Gelatine | Gelatin |
| Groundnut oil | Peanut oil |
| Icing | Frosting |
| Icing sugar | Confectioners' sugar |
| Lean bacon | Canadian bacon |
| Streaky bacon | American bacon |
| Omelette | Omelet |
| Orange, lemon rind/peel | Orange, lemon zest |
| Peeled shrimps | Shelled shrimps |

| | |
|---|---|
| Pimento | Pimiento |
| Plain chocolate | Semi-sweet chocolate |
| Plain flour | All-purpose flour |
| Pork back | Fat back |
| Round — or short-grain rice | Short-grain rice |
| Salt beef | Corned beef |
| Scones | Biscuits |
| Self-raising flour | All-purpose flour sifted with baking powder |
| Semolina | Semolina flour |
| Shredded beef suet | Chopped beef suet |
| Single cream | Half and half |
| Soft brown sugar | Light brown sugar |
| Spring onion | Scallion or green onions |
| Stem ginger | Preserved ginger |
| Sultanas | Seedless white raisins |
| Sweet | Candy |
| Vanilla pod | Vanilla bean |
| Vegetable marrow | Large zucchini/Marrow squash |
| Wholemeal | Wholewheat |

# Some equipment and terms

| English | American |
|---|---|
| Pastry case or flan | Pie shell |
| Baking tin | Baking pan |
| Base | Bottom |
| Cocktail stick | Toothpick |
| Mixture | Batter |
| Frying pan | Skillet |
| Greaseproof paper | Wax paper |
| Grill | Broil |
| Icing | Frosting |
| Kitchen paper | Paper towels |
| Knock back dough | Punch down dough |
| Liquidiser | Blender |
| Mince | Grind |
| Mincer | Grinder |
| Muslin | Cheesecloth |

| | |
|---|---|
| Patty cases | Patty shells |
| Pipe, using a *plain star-tube* in a *piping* bag | Pipe, using a *fluted nozzle* in a *pastry* bag |
| Stoned | Pitted |
| Whip/Whisk (eggs and cream) | Beat/Whip |

# Editor's Introduction

For the past two years I have lived in a state of near schizophrenia: who am I? Louisa Trotter, Rosa Lewis (on whose life The Duchess is based), the brilliant Gemma Jones, who portrayed Louisa, or a mixture of all three? And in this mixture just how much of Smith himself am I in turn imposing on those three characters and their work? Insofar as my own actual technical work in the making of *The Duchess of Duke Street* is concerned, there is no question that research, plus my own cookery skills have been married in an effort to produce for viewers dishes and scenes and sets which were 'authentic' and which looked evocative of the period when on screen.

None of this was as simple as it may sound; culinary montages — telling in pictures what cannot, or is not, said in words — take weeks of planning together with the individual writers, designers, prop buyers and directors of each particular episode. Sometimes the kitchen and dining-room scenes were important *per se*. Louisa Trotter actually cooking, together with her staff, and the dialogue related to what was

17

going on in the episode or scene. At other times the kitchen was a background against which a different story was being played out. Nevertheless, hotel kitchens are busy places and in a perpetual state of change, therefore no matter what the dialogue might be between characters, if this is being acted out in the Bentinck kitchens then the background activities had to be logical and chronologically accurate. Morning, noon, or evening? Breakfast, luncheon or dinner ? Each member of the cast would be given an interesting job to do. And each 'Extra' had to be trained by me to do whatever job had been selected for him or her to do: churning ice-cream, drawing and plucking fowls (they hated that!), straining soups, tammy-ing sauces or just simple chopping or peeling. All this gave an authentic feel to the scene — even to the point of injecting steam and smoke onto the sets when a *'point de service'* was imminent and the hustle, bustle and histrionics of 'dishing up' had to be shown.

Another aspect might perhaps be where the actual food was the key point, like in the early part of the first series when Louisa had lost all her money and had to turn her hand to making those hundreds of chicken and ham pies.

Here the scene had to show her effort, and eventual exhaustion.

A tremendous amount of pre-planning went into this episode, resulting in a complex of what I can only describe as 'culinary choreography' as we built up the complicated montages which showed Louisa actually using every ounce of energy and skill: hand-raising pies by the hundred, all at different stages of preparation, showing them actually being raised around wooden pie moulds, then filled with meats, lids fitted, decorations applied, edges pinched, pastry being egg-washed, then the hurry and scurry of tray upon tray of pies being pushed into the ovens, pulled out, stacked, filled with jelly, wrapped, trayed and delivered — all leading to her eventual collapse onto the floor due to the strain of it all. And all this had to be conveyed in approximately two minutes of edited film! It took us two eighteen-hour days to do this, and that is not counting the many planning meetings, rehearsals, and cooking preparations in my own kitchen in South-West London! A brave effort for all of us, but it paid off as this episode became a great talking point with the public.

Yet another side is the romantic and emotional setting, best suggested when Louisa's 'Love Swan' made its début.

This delicious confection consisted of a rich vanilla ice-cream swan atop a nest of baby meringues dripping with caramel, and appeared surrounded by gondolas of blazing brandied cherries, all set on an exquisite silver tray. The table where it was to make its appearance was itself a dream swagged with a garlands of multi-coloured Spring flowers; the tablecloth a frothy veil of creamy French organdie, all quite romantic and all devised and thought out to slot comfortably into the atmosphere of the eventual love scene between Louisa and Charlie Haslemere. The lighting alone of this scene was an artistic 'coup' and a great credit to the lighting designers. This episode was a pure delight to confect and assemble, but was certainly not without its hazards. How to keep the ice-cream chilled whilst waiting for the scene to be shot and the temperature in the studios at over 100°F? How could we keep the cherries blazing for fifteen minutes with an assistant cramped in the 'wings' ready to hand the whole assemblage to Gemma Jones as though it really had come straight from the Bentinck kitchens? Having Gemma Jones as the star of the show — totally professional — did help in no small way, as did instant potato for ice-cream and cotton wool pads soaked in methylated spirits hidden under mounds of Morello cherries to keep them ablaze!

Other 'nice ones to do' are those scenes where a situation has to be spelt out to viewers in a few seconds of camera 'crabbing', as in Episode 2 of the first series where at Lady Markham's luxurious Eaton Square house, wealth and opulence had to be implied.

Pyramids of exotic fruits on gilt tazzas — a very 'visual' technique — hoops and garlands composed of hundreds of roses and yards of smilax were used on the table (well, a scant dozen flower heads and a sprig of fern are not likely to give viewers much of an idea). All of which had to be wired, mossed and arranged. The heavily-laden table, spread with a linen cloth bordered with deep lace flouncing, was set and laid exactly as it would have been in such a household at the turn of the century: intricately folded napkins, a whole forest of cut crystal wine glasses, rows of silver cutlery arranged with military precision, crested gilt base plates, taper sticks with silk shades, hand-written menu cards, cellars, coasters, cruets and decanters. All of these would take a normal household staff of butlers, footmen and maids a day to prepare but had to be done by me and one assistant in four short hours, for rarely can we get into the studios on the day of filming before eight-thirty a.m., and there are always the added physical complications of five cameras and their attendant crews, sound booms, make-up staff, prop-men, directors, floor managers and those infernal cables, like hanks of knitting wool to manoeuvre and climb over and round — and all for a few seconds' film. But every penny spent, every nerve-end strained is worthwhile for the quality of the series.

In and amongst all this work I found (from the feedback on set by the actors) there was often an excellent opportunity to get many technical tips and hints of a culinary nature over to the viewer. Ideas which I have since learned they were quick to notice and appreciate, as in the scene where Louisa instructs (in no uncertain language) Mrs Wellkin, her cook, how to rectify a 'split' or curdled mayonnaise. In one brief thirty second shot you actually had a full cookery lesson — and again when Mrs Cochrane, head cook at the Bentinck (played by Mary Healey), has problems in getting her aspic to set, whilst on an outside catering job at an Ascot house in *midsummer* without any ice *apparently* available (these script writers made nervous wrecks of my little team, but what a deal of interesting historical fact we wove into some of the scenes together). Ice-houses, ice-boxes, ice men delivering — Louisa had that problem solved in two seconds. Many people didn't realise just how early electric refrigeration arrived in London — but the country used the old techniques. However *we* didn't. Still during that blistering summer of 1976 at Wood Lane (BBC Studios) even if we'd had an Arctic of ice there was no way our aspic was going to be controlled for that *pièce de boeuf en gelée!* Timing of shots is just not compatible to cookery requirements. Treacle — viscous and exactly the right colour for a rich Madeira jelly — solved the problem. It was this realisation, from the cast and the eventual feedback from viewers, that there was so much other than visual food which was of interest to them. Hence this book taking the form it does.

Mercifully for me Louisa Trotter (alias Rosa Lewis) never wrote a book. This left me totally free to interpret how she might have expressed things had she done so.

In her early years she was heavily influenced by the French (as was Rosa Lewis and indeed I, myself). An English chauvinism, however, grew within her fairly rapidly, as viewers are bound to have observed! I find this totally understandable and relate readily, not only with the character of Louisa Trotter but also with the legendary Rosa and maintain as they both do that much which comes from the stoves of France could well be left on that side of the Channel, leaving room for good English recipes, particularly those which gave the Bentinck its reputation for excellence.

Louisa's whole attitude to life was British, from the way she ran the Bentinck Hotel as a country house, a home from home for her clients, to the classic simplicity of her famous Quail Pudding. A masterpiece which even the great Auguste Escoffier acknowledged but went on to ruin in Louisa's eyes by, 'mucking about with it: upsetting the bleedin' flavour of me quail with too much other stuff'. Escoffier's version was far too Frenchified for Louisa's taste.

Always truthful to the point of bluntness, often (though wrongly) interpreted by those who don't understand this kind of character, as rudeness. Helpful, abundantly creative and inventive, scrupulously fair and, underneath, totally sensitive to the needs, feelings and conditions of all who had the privilege of coming into contact with her — particularly those who worked for her — who else would have retained that near-geriatric head waiter, Merriman, or tolerated the arrogance of Starr, the hall porter, not to mention the eccentric licence in permitting his dog Fred to patrol the front hall of the hotel?

In this book I have virtually become Louisa Trotter because I identify with her in so many ways, not least in my acceptance that I consider a basic French training as second to none, but, that over, I reserve the right to wave the British flag and promote what I think is good, no matter what its origins. So to this end I have collated some of my ideas and borrowed and bent recipes from other cooks of the period, not only to give the book an Edwardian atmosphere, but because I think they are good things as they stand.

Today's cook hostesses will, I hope, get inspiration for contemporary entertaining and for the non-cooks I trust there will be enough interest in the text to bring back delicious memories of *The Duchess* where they were taken by the cameras into kitchen, dining-room and parlour of the now legendary Bentinck.

*Michael Smith,*
*London 1977*

# Louisa Trotter's Introduction

When it comes to food, there's nobody more serious than me, and there's nobody knows better who's who and what's what when it comes to the best. I can tell a yarn or two and well-embroidered at that, but I won't — not here anyway. But to say I'd thought up *all* these recipes myself would be stretching it a bit. So before starting, I'd like to tell you a bit about my friends who are in the same line of business and what have helped me to become 'la reine de la cuisine' or the Queen of Cooks, as Monsieur Alex used to say in his better-tempered moments. He didn't half scare me when I first started at Lord Henry Norton's house in Curzon Street, you know; but it was him what really got my roots planted right, so to speak, and I'll always be grateful to him.

Of course, I used to read magazines and cookery books before getting my hands on the pans, and there was one lovely writer whose book I enjoyed more than anybody else's, propped up in my iron bed in the attic at my Mum and Dad's house in Wanstead. It was Miss Eliza Acton's *Modern Cookery*

'Monsieur Alex and Augustus Trotter discuss the menu at Lord Henry Norton's house.'

*in all its Branches.* This book is still about, and I'd recom-
mend it to any young lady what's starting out in life as a cook:
private or professional. She wrote sensible, informative stuff,
though her style got a bit fancy for me at times. She has a few
French ideas in her book; they say she was engaged at one time
to marry a Frenchman. And they also say she got put in the
family way, like I did with Charlie Haslemere. (Well, we know
her sister Sarah had several children, and the eldest one,
called Susannah, used to kiss Eliza's picture each night when
she went to bed, saying: 'She is the only mother I have known',
and that's maybe what got that story started); but the main
thing about her was, what with her trips to France and her
quick pen and even quicker mind, she thought up the idea of
*listing* all the ingredients needed in the making of a dish.
Before that, recipes used to mention the ingredients as they
went along, all jumbled up with instructions like. She made
for a good read, and she was logical, precise and tidy — all
that a woman cook should be. I can't abide sloppiness.

I'd have probably got on a lot better with Eliza as a person
— though she sounds a bit prudish — than with that Isabella
Beeton. *She* was a grand one, that one. She couldn't have
cooked all she talked about, well not in that little semi-
detached house in Pinner. Mind you, with a publisher
husband like Sam Beeton, it wouldn't have been too difficult
to get her book published, would it! I suppose that's just a
touch of the old sour grapes. She *did* know about society
though, and its goings-on. I learned everything about servants
and their jobs in private households from her book (*The Book
of Household Management,* 1861), and many's the table
setting I've copied from her illustrations and many the flower
arrangement I've used — until better ideas of my own came
up. Like I said, her recipes aren't all my sort. I think she was
frightened by a pint of cream, and there's too much preaching
and prattling about manners for my liking. I've got to admit
though that her English cakes is excellent and I always use
them for my teas, and I've included quite a few of them in this
book, a bit altered sometimes; but the basics are hers.

Now Agnes Marshall's another kettle of fish, if you'll pardon
the turn of phrase! *There's* one who gets her pinny on and her

sleeves rolled up! Whenever I had a new girl starting at the Bentinck, she was shipped off to Agnes' school in Mortimer Street. Saved Mrs Cochrane's nerves a lot of wear and tear, that did. It's the best cookery school in London, and all we had to do after they'd had a stint with her was lick them into our shape at the Bentinck.

Of course, when it comes to it, my two old friends Auguste Escoffier and César Ritz are the fellers really capable of reaching the heights, like what we have always aimed for in Duke Street. Not that we ever went in for all that fancy architectural stuff they thought up — just that the French still have the best foundations for a good kitchen.

Marie-Louise and César Ritz became great pals of mine — she was a lovely lady. I used to go and have tea with them when they opened their new hotel on Piccadilly in 1905. You see, we had similar ideas about what a hotel should be — like a house or a home. Not that you could compare the Bentinck with his beautiful new place. First steel-framed building in London was the Ritz Hotel, they tell me.

César was always very busy — their company had hotels all over Europe — I've stayed in most of them too. The Grand in Monte Carlo; the Ritz on the Place Vendôme in Paris, even got as far as Salsomaggiore to his Grand Hotel des Termes, *and* he tried to get me out to Budapest where he'd opened another Ritz. He was taken poorly at the time and Marie-Louise was having to do it all herself — but I reckon nothing much to those Central European countries — too hot-blooded for me. Look what happened to the Archduke Ferdinand in Sarajevo — got shot at didn't he? Caused a war as we all know — so I didn't go.

I went off to Paris with her a time or two though; in fact it was *me* what introduced *her* to the *Maison Blanc* where I got all my white muslin curtains made up. But no names woven on for the Bentinck, like they had at the Ritz.

No names nor badges on the silver neither. Nor on the china. Makes it too much like a hotel and less like a home.

Folk often marvelled that I got on with those two — them being Swiss and full of foreign ideas, but César's ideas on how to run international hotels were better than anybody's. I'd have put my money in his companies any day. Wally (Waldorf Astor) tried to get him to America, but he never went, not that I knew of anyway.

César would disagree with me in his gentlemanly way, never lifted his voice, not like me. 'Louisa,' he'd say, 'I am quite sure Crêpes Suzette would not be so much esteemed if they were not served with so much ceremony' — and then I'd remind him that it was his pal Escoffier what invented them! and that's why even old weary britches (Merriman) used to have a go with them in our private dining-rooms. Earned him a good tip or two did a showy-made Crêpe Suzette.

'You foreign cooks,' I'd tell him when we were talking about food, which we usually were, 'are a bit apt to "squeeze" your food, you're rather apt to take the juice out of the beef and put something else in' — and I'd watch him give a little wry smile. He knew that their French meat and chickens and game weren't as good as ours, their vegetables were better because they don't go in for the Harvest Festival-size stuff like what we do, and of course he knew that they were still the best *cooks* in the world.

An English gardener will grow a gooseberry 'til it's as big as your bleedin' head. The French like to get stuff on their plates *early*. In England we're *gardeners* and like to leave everything *on the tree;* we hate to pick flowers or dig up potatoes or anything.

The average 'Froggie' is a *market* gardener. Your English gardener is employed by the aristocracy to make the place beautiful to look at; the Frenchman cuts it off when it's small and crisp and full of flavour — what they call 'primeur' — and he gets a hell of a big price for it, particularly when he ships it over to our Covent Garden markets and dealers.

I think the Americans — from the South — enjoy their food and cook it well. It was a darkie cook from Savannah what taught me to cook rice. Mosianna was Willy Lowe's cook — right old American Colonial nobs they were — and the first Virginia hams ever cooked in London were brought over by him on the White Star Line together with American pepper-corns and brandy peaches; Willy Lowe sent me them to cook for 'Himself' (H.M.), him being a friend of his, and I'd prepare them like what I'd been shown out there.

I even had canvasback ducks sent from Rhode Island, and waffles with Vermont maple syrup to put on them. Put them on the Bentinck's breakfast menu, they proved to be a right novelty. And that was at the turn of the century too. Sweet potatoes were a Louisa Trotter pièce de résistance, and introduced early, because of our American clientèle at the hotel. Mather and Rudd eventually started stocking all this stuff, so I didn't have to bother getting it sent over special no more. This pleased Willy Lowe and Wally Astor.

As you will see from the contents of this book, I have strong feelings for the best ingredients used in the simplest ways, and this brings a lot of good English stuff with it. There's nothing wrong with that, as long as you remember that English roasts and puddings won't wait for no one, that's why dinners and lunches can't wait, and that's one reason why we don't have a public restaurant at the Bentinck. Though I still do like to get down to some of those French classical dishes which please me and my foreign-minded customers and which I can mix in with the best of what we've got here in London. But there's too much wine in some of them, hides the real flavour of the food, I think. I've argued this with those two Frenchmen 'til I'm blue in the face, and we just have to agree to differ. (The French'll never admit there's a deal of disguising done at times!) I did a stint in France, so I know. Worked for the Comte de Paris's lot for a time, in Paris, and Monsieur Alex wasn't against a side step or two every now and then — I noticed, got eyes in the back of my head, I have!

Then, we've got to get cleared up the difference between the classical French kitchen and the Provincial one. I always say the best of France comes from the stoves of the women out in the provinces; places like Lyons, Tours, Angoulême, Brest and Dijon, and up in those hills in Provence with all those herbs, and where all the apples and cream come from in Normandy — mind you, not that I've been to these spots, but I heard when I was in Paris. I'm very grateful to the French — 'cos aren't they the only ones what'll have women in their kitchens? *and* give them the respect they deserve?

I'm still the only woman chef in England and I can't see

there being much change yet for a bit. Too chauvinistic our men are — and what for? They can't cook, most of 'em. It's not in the nature of Englishmen. That's why we rely on the Frogs and Krauts and Ities, isn't it? There's a bit too much of the Old Raj about for my liking, in London in particular, had too much slaving done for them at school by their fags and in the army there was their batmen. But it'll change one day, you'll see.

I've always had *girls* at the Bentinck and always will have. But the times aren't right in London to mix the sexes (not at me stoves that is!) — so we remain an island. The men laugh at us, 'til they've tasted our dishes that is, and then the laugh's on them. There's a deal of jealousy about when we get asked to do dinners in the big houses — and we've been at the Admiralty and the Colonial Office as well — and when Kaiser Bill was staying at Christchurch Castle, who do you think got asked to look after his little lot? — my French friends? Not on your life: The Queen of Cooks, Louisa Trotter, no less, and of course Society's always followed what I've started; well, with H.M. bestowing so much favour around what else could they do?

It was me what started serving bacon and egg breakfasts after balls and suppers, and I introduced those little cushions they carried everywhere when they were meeting and flirtin' in the back passages and on the stairs of the big houses. I always say 'a thoroughbred does and knows what's right *instinctively!*' and the real nobs knew I had some right ideas.

But they always wanted something different when I went out to cook for them. Waldorf Astor at Hever Castle in particular. It was him what persuaded me to go to America. We had a lot of American clients at the hotel, they liked the English country house atmosphere I'd built into it. I used to kill me own turtles and make me own turtle soup then tin it for them to take back, they liked that I can tell you! Yes, there'd always to be something different going on; that's why I brought these things from America to England: to keep my clients interested all the time.

Any woman can cook better than any man — there's those who'll have my guts for garters for saying it, but it's true and they know it — (and you women know it's true; where's the best cooking done in this country? — in the homes!). And why are some people's dishes better than others? Because some people have more life in them — more vitality, more guts than others.

Anybody without these can never make food taste right. No matter what materials you give them, it's no use. Turn in the whole cowful of cream instead of milk, and it'll still taste dull and flabby because they've nothing in themselves to give; no *feeling for food.* And perhaps what's more important, you've got to like eating. I don't trust no cook or chef what won't eat their own cooking. Makes for good sense, doesn't it?

Then you've got to look after them what help you — work for you. You can't treat them like machines. Give them good food and comfortable rooms. Give them pianos to play on if they want to, and send them off to theatres and concerts. Make life pleasant for them. They have their lives to live like the rest of us.

I always try to have good-looking girls in my kitchens — attractive to the eye — and all beautifully dressed; spotless, always in white. I even have special white buttons made for their frocks and aprons, and specially made they all are at Marshall & Snelgrove (who thought they was lowering themselves when I first asked them to do these). Makes them feel proud to be cooks it does, and of course it all adds to my good reputation, doesn't it?

So to sum up: do your own marketing down to the last potato; treat your guests well; treat your staff well; always think up something different; and always make sure everything's *beautiful,* from the way you're turned out yourself right down to the last flower and glass on the table.

Put a bit of life into your entertaining, right to the very finish, and to this end I give you the benefit of my advice in the book, and remain, just like I began, plain Louisa Trotter — cook.

*Bentinck Hotel,*
*Duke Street,*
*London, S. W.*

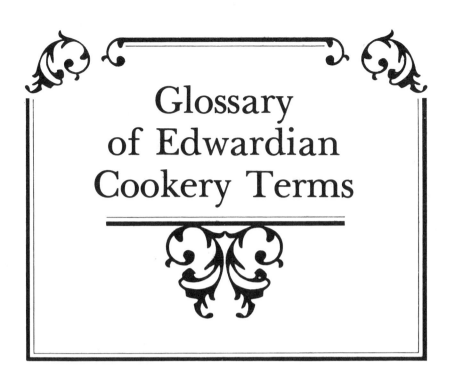

# Glossary of Edwardian Cookery Terms

Agnes Marshall being, like I said, a good pal of mine, gets trusted with teaching some of my girls their first steps (she then sends me *her* best girls to get a bit of spit and polish when they get onto proper 'cuisine').

I've never had no time, nor patience, to write down all what I learned, but I remember when I first started with Monsieur Alex at Lord Henry Norton's place, the first thing he made me do was learn all the French terms so that I could understand French cookery books and menus. I was always glad later on that I did, particularly when Auguste Escoffier used to send me some of his best recipes, as he only wrote in French, like what chefs all do, and any recipes I cadged from Tschumi at the Palace they'd be in French as well, so let's get this list over and done with.

I burned many a candle memorising my cooking terms, so 'Learn it' is what I tell my girls, 'and you'll never be stuck.'

'My kitchens at the Bentinck.'

*Note: Editor's comments in brackets*

*Ambigu* A meal where all the courses are placed on the table at once, such as high tea, breakfasts, etc.

*Aspic* Clear savoury jelly used for garnishing.

*Attelets* Skewers either of wood, iron, or electroplate. In this latter case they replace either of the former when dishing up, as in kabobs (kebabs) etc.

*Au Bleu* Term used for fish stewed in wine. (Now means cooked live in court bouillon).

*Au Jus* Any dish dressed with its own gravy or meat stock.

*Baba* A very light Polish cake (made of light yeast dough).

*Béarnaise* A sauce prepared like Hollandaise sauce, but flavoured with tarragon and herbs — (often said to have had its origins in Béarn).

*Béchamel* A white sauce. (Made with butter, flour and aromitised milk).

*Beignets* Fritters.

*Bisque* A kind of thick soup made of shellfish. (The 'biscuit' being the thickening agent.)

*Blanch* To blanch. To put vegetables etc. in cold water and bring to the boil, to remove any bitter taste or to facilitate the cleansing — *and then to plunge into cold water: this helps retain colour.*

*Blanquette* A fricassée of white meat served with a rich white sauce thickened with yolk of egg (and cream).

*Bouillon* Broth, (common) stock, or (clear) soup.

*Braise* To stew anything very slowly (in liquid) with vegetables, herbs etc. in a tightly-covered pan.

*Braisière* A braising-pan made for the above purpose.

*Broche A la broche,* (spit) roasted.


*Caisses* The little paper cases in which various things, such as farced (stuffed) larks, chaudfroid of quails etc. are served.

*Canapé* Fried croûton *or piece of bread, biscuit or pastry* on which various savoury titbits are served.

*Casserole* A stewpan.

*Compôte* Fruit stewed or steeped in syrup.

*Coquilles* Shells. Shell-shaped dishes, such as scalloped oysters etc. are served in.

*Cutlets* The chops from the best end of neck of mutton (lamb), trimmed, and served in various ways. The name is also applied to other meats and vegetables dished up in the shape of mutton cutlets — mutton (or lamb) — shape of mutton (or lamb).


*Entremêts* Dishes either sweet or savoury, served at second course. (Now most usually implying sweet dishes at the end of a meal).


*Filet* Mutton (lamb), or venison; the sliced undercut of sirloin of beef and the corresponding parts of veal, mutton, or venison; the thick slices on each side of the spine in hares and rabbits; the breasts of poultry or game. In fish, the flesh lifted clear off the backbone on both sides, freed from skin and bone, and cut into neat pieces.

*Fricassée* Poultry (veal) or fish cut into neat pieces and served with a (rich) white sauce; may be garnished with truffles, mushrooms, etc.

*Friture* The substance, whether oil, butter, lard, or dripping, in which fish, fritters etc are fried. Also the receptacle in which these are fried.

*Galantine* Meat or poultry boned and stuffed with forcemeat, truffles etc., braised or boiled, and when cold served (coated) with aspic jelly.

*Julienne* Clear soup with vegetables, such as leeks, carrots, turnips, celery etc. The vegetables are cut in shreds used for this soup.

*Kabobs* (Kebabs) Small and highly seasoned pieces of mutton (lamb), veal, or poultry, put on a skewer, either by themselves or alternately with slices of onion, bacon, etc., and either grilled, fried or roasted, and served with different sauces.

*Kedgeree* An Indian dish of already cooked fish, rice, eggs, and seasoning, usually served for breakfast in England.

*Lard* To pass thin strips of fat bacon through meat, such as *fricandeau* or *grenadins;* or through the breasts of poultry, game etc. This must be neatly and evenly done *with* the grain in beef, veal etc., *across* it in poultry, game etc.

*Marinade* A sort of pickle generally composed of oil, vinegar, or lemon juice, wine, seasoning etc., in which meat and fish are sometimes steeped to heighten their flavour.

*Mayonnaise* A cold emulsion sauce of egg yolks, oil and vinegar.

*Meringue* A light sort of 'pastry' (sic) made with white of egg and sifted sugar, usually served as cases for cream, ice, etc.

*Mirepoix* A highly concentrated sauce, almost a glaze, strongly flavoured with vegetables, wine and spice, used for many entrées, etc. (Now means a bed of mixed vegetables on which to roast a joint etc.)

*Panard* (Panada or Panade) A mixture of butter, flour, water, and salt, slowly cooked, an ingredient used in various kinds of farces and forcemeat.

*Pâté* A pie, usually of a special and rich kind. (Also a savoury meat or fish paste.)

*Paupietta* (Paupiettes) or Polpetti. Square thin piece of meat or fish rolled round various kinds of forcemeat, sliced into shape, usually wrapped in a thin slice of fat bacon, egged and breadcrumbed, and fried and served with various sauces.

*Petits Fours* Small (almond) pastry, served at dessert.

*Pilau* (Pilaf) An Eastern stew, usually served with rice, curry, and hot condiments. (Now means the rice itself.)

*Poach* To boil (without movement) in water or stock.

*Quenelles* Small shapes of uncooked fish, veal, poultry, or any white meat, pounded and mixed with panard (panade), eggs and cream, then poached in stock.

*Roux* A thickening of butter and flour (two-thirds former to one-third latter), allowed to colour over the fire or not, according as it is wanted for white or brown sauce.

*Soufflé* A very light (risen) pudding, either savoury or sweet.

*Suprème* A very rich white sauce, composed of essence of chicken, Velouté sauce, fresh mushroom etc. An entrée of the best parts of (breasts) the fowl, chicken, etc.

# Louisa Trotter
# on Marketing

There was a time, right back in eleven hundred and something, when Smithfield was 'a plain grassy space just outside
the city walls' — a *smooth field*, get it? — where things weren't
just confined to the purveying of meat, but archery and
tournaments was held there for the interest of the city
dwellers; and if you'd misdemeaned, then you got your head
chopped off, well hanged it was in them days, *and* you could
be burnt at the stake for any fancy religious beliefs you might
have thought up and put into practice!

It's a bit different today. The world comes here to buy its
meat and near on two thousand men run the place. The cattle
market got moved out to Islington in 1855 I'm told, as there
wasn't room for them, and even then they've had to build two
new sections, the most recent one where they've put the poultry
and game, was opened in 1899. I got asked along to the special
opening party with all the other nobs. That was a day I can
tell you — a right booze-up we had.

'. . . get to the market early.'

If you're ever round there at five o'clock in the morning — winter or summer, come hell or high water makes no odds — you'll as like as not find me in the Cock Tavern drinking a mug of 'wazzer' (whisky and tea) with the bummarees (carrying porters). I know who to keep the right side of in this life.

There was a time, when the Bentinck wasn't doing so good, when I pushed my own barrow back to the hotel loaded with meat, chickens, pheasants and such like. But not no more — costs me a bob, but they'll do anything for me, will those porters. They know me well enough to give me the best service and top quality stuff.

They say bad habits die hard; I'll say that for good ones as well. Monsieur Alex learnt me right at the beginning to get up, get out, and get picking and choosing. You can't do with bad stuff being foisted off on to you, for the sake of getting out of bed a bit early. 'The best quality raw materials, my girl,' he said, and only the best will do today for yours truly.

I'll admit that these days — unless I've got a special dinner to cook myself — I'll only go round two or three times a week.

After Smithfield I like to nip on to Billingsgate to pick my fish, and then I like to end up last at Covent Garden. When you think that it was once the garden of a nunnery, Co(n)vent Garden, it pulls you up sharp. But it's still a garden, isn't it? Row after row of beautiful vegetables and flowers in a million different colours, just like a mosaic it looks. And the smell — a bit different from Billingsgate, that's for sure!

Mind you, they're a crafty lot some of them, all the biggest and the best, prettied up to catch your eye, and they'll as soon have a yesterday's cauliflower in your bag as wink. 'Let me feel them stalks,' I say, if they don't snap brittle, they can have 'em back. I don't want none of these limp-stalked caulies — crisp, white and firm as a young woman's breasts for the Bentinck. *And* they know it!

I've learnt a lot, the hard way too. But in the end it's the best way. Nobody can't fool nobody then, can they? And you build up a mutual trust; once they know you'll pay the top price for top stuff they soon see you get it.

That's the way I started marketing, and that's the way I do it to this day.

'Choosing my own quail.'

# Louisa Trotter
# on Table Settings

Most of the upper middle classes were half crazy with snobbery at the turn of the century, and we got our share of them at the Bentinck. Always trying to get themselves into the real top drawer, trying to mingle with the real quality — the aristocracy and the old landed families or 'county set'.

They'd plenty of money and they paid for what they got — Ascot, Henley, extravagant house-parties what me and my girls would cook up for them, and I got well paid — often as much as £50 a time for it, and the dinner would cost them as much as £1.7s.0d, a nob on top of that! Prices isn't cheap for London's 'Queen of Cooks', I can tell you. And them what had style — and we certainly had plenty of stylish people at the hotel — all the intellectuals, actors, writers but *NO* bleedin' reporters — they snoop and pry too much — nothing's private when they're around — would always want a Champagne supper in their opera box at Covent Garden. French silk table-cloths and serviettes they'd get if they had a good 'handle'

'I always do me own flowers.'

(title) to their names. Everything sent round in a cab and set up ready for the interval. And you couldn't forget nothing on these sort of trips — ice, cooled butter, special flowers. *And* they could have hot dishes if they liked, this is where my hay-boxes came in useful; the Opera House didn't have nothing in the way of facilities. But these sort of people, *my* sort of people, *beautiful* people (this expression is back in use today for the 'in set', though be it they often differ in background if not in shape, age, form and intelligence) always wanted, and got, the best whether at my hotel or in their own house.

Yet classes are open to anyone if you're prepared to climb the social ladder, and realise that it entails self-discipline and sacrifice (or you'll slip back to where you came from). I wasn't never going to do that — nor did I. I watched and copied and listened and read. I know that being pretty helped (certainly with H.M.), but if I hadn't been the best cook in London he wouldn't have had reason to notice me, so you never know where the door's going to open; always keep your apple-pies (eyes) open, and when it does, go through it and up those stairs (if you'll forgive the suggestion).

The dining-table was very much the catalyst on the social scene and where people could act out their snobberies and fantasies. No longer did they eat with the sexy gusto of the eighteenth century, where over-imbibing and over-eating was normal to the high-living Georgians.

In the nineteenth century the table had become a complex stage where a social charade was played out, and I knew this; and I played along with it whenever I could. Everything had to be as beautiful as possible. Didn't matter what it cost. If two hundred roses were right, then two hundred roses it was.

Silk shades on the candles. Elaborate silver epergnes draped with smilax and groaning with exotic flowers. Pyramids of hothouse apricots and candied sweetmeats. Six, seven and eight glasses at each place, and a forest of nonsense of silver knives, forks and spoons that foxed the cleverest of them — (knowing which to pick up for what). These were the days when you used both hands when eating — (the American stab-and-pick technique hadn't arrived in England, nor had the general acceptance of the cocktail, though Alexis Soyer had

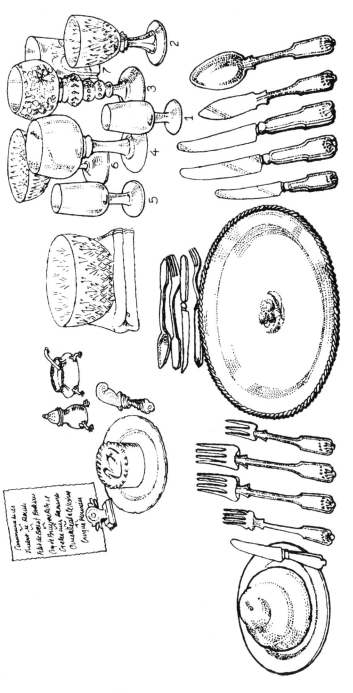

An Edwardian table setting

*l to r — Bottom Row:* side plate, side or butter knife, fish fork, entrée fork, relevée fork, savoury fork, silver crested base platter, savoury knife, relevée knife, entrée knife, fish knife, (English) soup spoon. *Across top of base platter:* dessert spoon and fork, fruit knife and fork. *Top row:* menu and menu holder, individual butter dish and knife, individual salt and pepper, finger bowl and napkin. *Glasses:* 1. Sherry 2. White wine 3. Moselle or Rhine wine 4. Claret or Burgundy 5. Port 6. Champagne 7. Tumbler

45

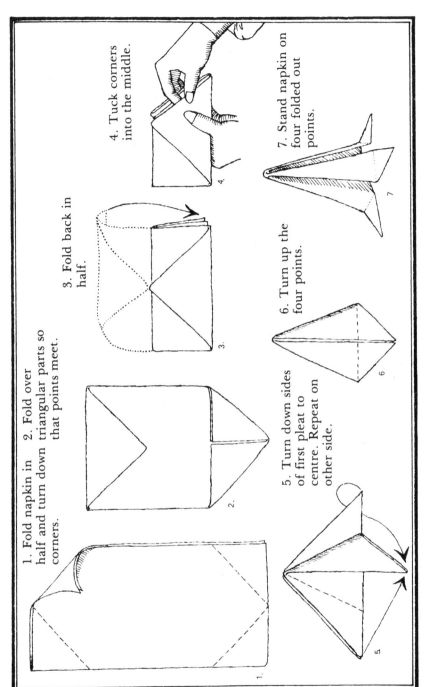

1. Fold napkin in half and turn down corners.

2. Fold over triangular parts so that points meet.

3. Fold back in half.

4. Tuck corners into the middle.

5. Turn down sides of first pleat to centre. Repeat on other side.

6. Turn up the four points.

7. Stand napkin on four folded out points.

How to make a Pyramid Napkin

46

introduced this mixed drink as long ago as 1855). You started your drinking later — *after* dinner, when the ladies left the men to it.

Base platters of crested silver were set at each place, at the hotel as well as in private houses. Merriman and his crew had all on to see that the silver was kept nice and bright. On top of twelve to fourteen pieces of cutlery for each guest there was a silver menu holder, individual salts, and often your own butter-dish and knife.

The tables, like I said, were very beautiful; I always saw to that myself. Then we had intricately folded napkins which would make the Japanese and their origami techniques look a bit sick. Fans, Boar's heads, Prince of Wales' feather, shoes and slippers — almost any shape. To me the pyramid (p. 46) takes a lot of beating and I always had them folded this way when H.M. the King was at table.

As soon as guests were seated — having been summoned by Merriman banging his sonorous old gong — the women started Act One. Off with their gloves — a finger at a time — the 'hands' then tucked neatly under the wrist and into the 'sleeve'.

Then you unfold your napkin — don't start tucking it in your chest or anywhere, that won't do — lay it across your lap. Have a quick peep at the menu and decide what you're going to miss out. It is always polite to refuse the odd course or two with a little gesture of your right hand to the butler or footman what's serving you (never called a waiter in a private house, and in the best households you don't have women either waiting at table. Liveried butlers and footmen only. H.M. wouldn't *never* have girls serving at any dinner table where he was, and we all knew that.)

Then watch out for all the social pitfalls. Do you know I've actually seen people what cut their bread with their knives! Break it, holding both hands over your side-plate to do this; don't want crumbs all over, do we?

Now there's many who think soup is for slurping. It takes a clever person to eat soup proper. And that tablespoon's not a table spoon, it's an English soup spoon! Take your soup nice and gentle from the *side* of the spoon's bowl. And don't never eat up, though in my hotel, or wherever I'm cooking up a dinner, I'd rather see an empty plate.

The Queen (Alexandra) brought a custom from her country (Denmark) what caught on for a little while, where you eat your fish with two forks. It's quite logical really, that is, much easier for coping with bones and skin and what not. But fish eaters have taken the place of that little bit of choreography. Again, remember, don't eat up. It's only the poor and greedy what eats up (unless you're at the Bentinck with Louisa Trotter, and then it's always too good to leave!)

I've seen some funny habits and manners in my time: some that make me laugh and there's some what just annoys me, and one of these habits is where folk will hold their knives and forks like they was writing a bleedin' letter or knitting. Get hold of them proper. The end of the handles tucked into the palm of your hand, your forefinger down the 'spine' of the knife and fork. This way you can *cut*. What do you think the knife blade's for?

It takes a few years' training to cope adequately with the fruit. But there aren't many débutantes who can't peel a peach or skin a banana with a knife and fork before they're wed! Grapes, tangerines, Muscatels and nuts you can use your hands for, but make sure the butler's brought a finger bowl before you start.

Quality people start their social training in the nursery, so you can see why it's difficult for folk to catch up when they come onto the social scene late.

Mind you — and this is something I've learnt — and a good piece of advice for all — if you behave natural and speak in your natural voice, nobody's going to notice much wrong. The real top class people won't never put anybody down; it's only them on their way up who feel insecure and nervous who behave badly.

Those with brains and ideas and thinking minds, no matter where they're from — could be Dukes, could be dustbin men — have created their own special élite clique and made themselves in demand at the dinner tables of the borin' lot, and it's for the likes of these that my stage is set. We've made some right shows at the hotel. We had one party — after Ascot it was — out in the courtyard. I had a special fountain built in the middle, the buffet table built round it. (Got that idea from Louis XIV when he gave a banquet in the courtyard at Versailles.) Covered all the table tops with roses — hundreds of them — a right picture that was.

In the private houses and mansions where we used to cook up dinners, we'd use all their own stuff. Lady Markham's was one of my favourite places. She had a lovely house. Everything Crown Derby or Minton and silver gilt and Waterford Crystal.

I made my first fruit pyramids there of apricots and blue plums and little bay leaves. They stood two feet high when I'd finished, and we had *eight* of them on the tables. It looked a real picture. Gold candlesticks with little cream silk shades went down each side of her table, and three of the nicest epergnes I've ever had my hands on were dressed up with apricot-coloured roses and carnations and leaves of all sorts. They stood as high as three church spires down the middle. I thought up a new idea and made my first flower 'hoops' linking everything together. Mind you, you couldn't see across the table hardly. But then you didn't need to. You talked to the lady or gentleman on your left or right; that's why it's important for a hostess to know who her guests are and place them proper. It took a lot of thought, and woe betide any new bride what got it wrong!

An eye for detail, I tell my girls, and check on everything.

Many a time people didn't want their houses messing up with a party — and the fashion of hiring hotels and restaurants wasn't really started — so I'd find an empty house and tart it up. I had plenty of friends in the good antique furniture trade and I'd borrow everything in a night: tables, chairs, side-tables, pictures, right down to the curtains. The place looked just like a real home. Build on a silk-lined marquee (tent) if it was a grand affair. Tapestry carpets on the stairs and floors even and just for a night.

Louisa Trotter knew how to do things; then I'd hire butlers and footmen, put them into the best liveries, and nobody knew they wasn't in a private home.

Me and my girls would move in and cook up one of my special supper menus and next day, come twelve o'clock, nobody knew that anything had gone on; the house would be as empty as a flag day in Aberdeen.

They got the lot when they asked me to do a party for them; and they all came to me, Dukes, Earls, actors, the nouveau riche — like I said, the lot and — if I liked them — I'd do anything for them, but I had to like them.

Get your stage right, and you're a winner. And having got your 'set' designed, stick to it. Don't chop and change about just for the sake of it; everybody gets nervous and you don't want that. Too much fainting about the place is inconvenient, so make your plans early; discuss it all with your cook, house-keeper and butler, then leave them to it. Bawl them out later if it's necessary, never in front of other people. Lose their respect this way, and the well-earned respect of your staff is essential to the good running of a house or a business.

These are a few of my ideas from the Bentinck for you to put into practice in your own homes next time you're entertaining. With a bit of practice you'll soon master most of it so that it comes as easy as falling off a wall.

'Grapes and camellias . . .' The Duchess at her inventive best — a beautiful dinner-table setting.

# Breakfast Dishes
# & Savouries

England has built its reputation on its breakfasts, it's the one meal that foreigners enjoy, too, because we do it so well.

At the Bentinck the breakfast table was always most important; if any guests wanted it in bed, they could have it in bed, on a big tray fitted with little drop-down legs; but usually they would have their baths and put on their peignoirs or dressing-gowns and we'd wheel in the tables for them. I'd had these tables made special, to fit the corridors and to go through the doors of the sets (suites) of rooms. When Merriman and his men had got them inside there was a nice broad flap to lift up, giving plenty of room to move. They all had white cloths with deep lace borders and serviettes to match, a different pattern for each set of rooms we had. White always looks nice and crisp and fresh first thing in the morning, doesn't it? A big posy of fresh flowers — done special each morning, mind you; my housekeepers didn't stand idle letting cobwebs grow on them, I can tell you — was on each setting, and the silver sparkled like the Koh-i-Noor diamond and if it didn't I wanted to know why.

'Making me first omelette.'

Old Misery (Merriman) knew to find out what papers they all read — it was usually *The Times* — and the ladies liked a copy of *The London Gazette* or *The Bystander* to keep them amused — and that stood folded and put into a silver holder. Special little chafing-dishes and lamps kept everything hot, and of course there was a silver kettle and lamp for those what wanted tea, to make it fresh for themselves. Coffee was made by the old 'jug and spoon' method and then decanted piping hot into the silver pots. (I'm changing my mind about silver for coffee, I've started to use china — tastes better, I feel.)

Not having a dining-room at the hotel meant we couldn't have no cold buffet which was usual in the grand hotels and houses in London, and in the country. But we still managed to get a good variety of dishes to whet their appetites. Never got no complaints about my breakfasts.

Well, here's *some* of the things we liked to cook up for them: they always say the proof of a pudding's in the eating of it, so if you want to try a few new ideas, read on, and whilst we're about it, try and remember there's more to bread than plain white! — there's brown bread and rye bread, potato scones, oatcakes, and, I like to get French sometimes and make fresh brioches and croissants.

There was once when Mrs Cochrane started slipping a bit — I think she was having family trouble at the time, but her being a good Yorkshire woman she stood to her job. 'You need a bit of help, my girl,' said I, so I gave her my little *Breakfast Book* published in 1865 by Richard Bentley's lot. Over three hundred different dishes are in it — *three hundred,* mark you!

Well, I didn't expect Mrs C. to meet that at the Bentinck, but I told her, 'Just in case the old brain box is getting a bit dull, have a look at this' — and I've never had no bother since. Here's just a few of the bills of fare from that book to get you thinking.

# Spring Quarter

*Breakfast for 12 or more persons*

*Middle of the table*

Target of Lamb

*

*6 By-dishes, Cold*

| | |
|---|---|
| Pickled Gherkins | Preserved Tunny Fish |
| Fillets of Anchovies | Bayonne Goose |
| Potted Hare | Pickled Ox Palates |

*

*6 By-dishes, Hot*

Small Patties of Shrimps
Haunches of Rabbits,
*en papillotes*
Smoked Salmon, tossed
Lambs' Tongues, with Parmesan
Trout Cutlets, broiled
White Puddings, tossed

*

*4 Entrées*

| | |
|---|---|
| Veal Cutlets, tossed | Curried Chicken |
| Smelts, in cases (tartlets) | Duck Pie |

*

*2 Entremets*

| | |
|---|---|
| Omelette of Veal Kidney | Young Potatoes, *au naturel* |

*

Cream Cheese, Candied Fruit, etc. according to fancy

# Summer Quarter

*Breakfast for 12 or more persons*

*Middle of the Table*

Galantine of Veal
Marbled Veal

\*

*6 By-dishes, Cold*

Cold Meat, *en vinaigrette*        Potted Venison
Pickled Turkey        Oyster Loaves
Lobster Patties        Preserved Rabbit

\*

*6 By-dishes, Hot*

Calf's Liver, tossed        Pigeons, broiled
Kippered Mackerel        Croquette of Prawns
Coquilles of Fowl        Poached Eggs and Spinach

\*

*4 Entrées*

Perch, tossed        Poulet, *à la chipolata*
Raised Pie of Ham        Salad of Pike

\*

*2 Entremets*

Oysters and Macaroni        Artichokes, with Gravy

\*

Candied and Fresh Fruits, Biscuits, etc.

# Autumn Quarter

*Breakfast for 12 or more persons*

*Middle of the Table*

Partridges, roasted and glazed

\*

*6 By-dishes, Cold*

| | |
|---|---|
| Lyons Sausage | Pheasant Patties |
| Pickled Cockles | Marbled Veal |
| Potted cold boiled Beef | Canapés of Sardines |

\*

*6 By-dishes, Hot*

| | |
|---|---|
| Oyster Sausages | Game Puddings |
| Devilled Turkey | Polpettes of cold Meat |
| Ham Toast | Bloaters, tossed |

\*

*4 Entrées*

| | |
|---|---|
| Tench Pie | Rolled Goose |
| Grouse, *à la minute* | Terrine of Hare |

\*

*2 Entremets*

Truffles, *à la serviette*        Omelette of Mushrooms

\*

Biscuits, Marmalades, Bonbons, and the usual accessories.

# Winter Quarter

*Breakfast for 12 or more persons*

*Middle of the Table*

Imitated Boar's Head

*

*6 By-dishes, Cold*

Slices of cold Ham      Oyster Patties
Pickled Salmon      Cresses
Pork Cheese (Brawn)      *Petits Pâtés* of Trout

*

*6 By-dishes, Hot*

Marinade of Turkey
Sweetbreads, *en caisse* (in paper)
Game Toast
Devilled Rabbit
Dressed Crab
Mayonnaise of Turbot or Salmon

*

*4 Entrées*

Yorkshire Pie      Périgord Pie
Blanquette of Veal      Curried Mutton

*

*2 Entremets*

Omelette of Gruyère Cheese      Truffles, tossed

*

Accessories as usual

# Omelette

An omelette is really scrambled eggs enclosed in a coat of coagulated egg. To get at this you first need to follow one or two simple rules.

Beat 3 eggs, season with salt and pepper. Melt $\frac{1}{2}$ oz. of butter in a heavy bottomed omelette pan, swirling it round so that the butter melts evenly. Let it get hot enough to foam and give off a nutty smell, which makes the omelette taste a treat. Pour in the eggs which will 'seize' almost immediately if the butter's right. Using the 'back' of a fork, stir the eggs swiftly all over the bottom of the pan using a circular movement and getting right to the edges. As soon as the egg mass starts to set, stop stirring and start rolling it up. It's up to you how well done you like an omelette as to how long you leave it at this stage; before collecting it up into a nice shape.

Any filling is put in just before you finally flip it over onto a warm plate.

# Omelette Florentine

Fill the omelette with a purée of spinach bound with a little cream and well seasoned with ground nutmeg, salt and pepper.

# Omelette à la Lyonnaise

Add finely chopped onion to the pan and let it acquire a good brown colour before adding the egg mixture and making the omelette in the usual way.

# Omelette Major Farjeon

This was the way I cooked an omelette for Johnny when he stayed at the Bentinck the night before his wedding.

Fill the omelette with 2 spoons of creamed smoked haddock just before rolling it up. Make a slit down the 'spine' and fill this with tiny ($\frac{1}{4}$ inch) bread croûtons fried in butter and mixed with plenty of chopped parsley and chives.

# Poached Eggs

Fresh eggs — where the raw white appears to cling to the yolk — are essential when an egg is to be poached in a 'court-bouillon'. If your eggs are not fresh then you'll have to resort to one of those new-fangled pans with little dishes for each egg, or you can use lightly boiled and shelled eggs.

Bring to the boil some lightly salted water acidulated with a little wine vinegar. Break each egg into a cup and slide it into the pan. *Reduce the heat* and *simmer* for three minutes. Lift out the finished eggs with a slotted spoon; dip them into cold water, trim the whites neatly with a knife, and slide them back into warm water until ready to serve. Drain carefully of any water on a clean cloth.

# Poached Eggs Queen Victoria

Put a little chopped lobster into individual tartlet cases. Place an egg in each case, coat with lobster sauce to which chopped truffles have been added.

# Poached Eggs à La Clamart

Make individual pastry cases for each serving. Put in a spoonful of rather stiff but freshly made pea purée lightly seasoned with garlic and a modicum of nutmeg. Lay on the poached egg and coat with a little cream sauce into which you've beaten some of the pea purée to colour and flavour it nicely.

# Poached Eggs Argenteuil

Garnish the bottom of some tartlet-crusts with asparagus cut into pieces and cooked, and six green asparagus-heads, about $1\frac{1}{2}$ inches in length, arranged like a star. Place an egg, coated with cream sauce mixed with half its volume of asparagus purée, upon each tartlet.

# To Scramble Eggs

There's many people think they know how to scramble an egg, but I've had too many disasters in my time to be convinced of that for a fact; they're usually either over-cooked and dry, or watery. This is one dish you've got to do yourself. Mrs C. could manage but the kids had no idea what it was all about; they'd learn mind you, or they'd get a clip over the ear!

A scrambled egg to me is the nicest way of eating eggs — all creamy and buttery and fluffy and at their best when served plain on crisp buttered toast; but I give you a few notions to bring a bit of variety into your breakfast times when the old man's hidden behind his newspaper!

A man will need 3 eggs a serving, but it's up to you how generous you want to be, but don't skimp.

Take a heavy-bottomed pan, set it over a low heat and put in a good ounce of butter. Just let it melt. It mustn't get hot. Beat 6 eggs — not too much, mind — season with salt and a little bit of white pepper. Pour the eggs into the pan and leave things be for a minute or two.

Now you need a straight-edged spatula to 'draw' the eggs across the bottom of the pan — don't go scratching round with a fork, like a hen in a pen. Don't raise the heat either, as this will cause lumps to form and destroy the light texture you're aiming for; be patient — you can't hurry a good scrambled egg.

When they are just — and only just — set, take the pan from the heat and squeeze or dab over them an extra ounce of very soft butter and 2 tablespoons of thick cream. Stir everything round just once or twice and serve as quick as you like: it can't be too quick. Scrambled eggs won't wait for no-one, and you can't mess about doing other food neither. They need your full attention while they're cooking.

# Scrambled Eggs à La Bohemienne

Auguste Escoffier showed me this way: try it next time you have somebody special you want to do a treat for. You need one brioche for each serving. Cut off the tops and take out the crumb. Whilst you're scrambling your eggs, warm the brioche through in a 'low' oven. Put a slice of foie gras (mousse de foie will do, but it should be mild-flavoured) into each brioche. Chop some truffles into the eggs when you add the cream (see above), fill into the warm brioche.

# Scrambled Eggs Bentinck

This is a very special dish and is for use on Easter Day. It can also be served at lunchtime as a hot hors-d'oeuvre.

Make individual tartlet cases (3 to 4 inch diameter and $\frac{3}{4}$ inch deep) for each serving. Fill the bottoms with minced shrimps heated quickly in a tablespoon of thick cream. Pile on scrambled eggs, then cover each tartlet with a good inch thickness of cheese soufflé mixture. Make sure it covers the surface completely: (a piping bag without a nozzle will help here). Bake in a hot oven (Gas 7, Elec. 425 to 450°) 'til risen and brown. Serve immediately.

# Scrambled Eggs Ma-Mère

I called them this because we used to have them this way at home in Wanstead when we was kids.

Cut some slices of de-crusted white bread into tiny ($\frac{1}{4}$ inch) cubes. Fry them in butter 'til they're crisp and fold into scrambled eggs just before you serve them, so that the croûtons stay crunchy.

# Louisa Trotter's Kedgeree

There's many a battle been fought in many a kitchen about what should or should not be put into a kedgeree.

Mine's never done no-one no harm; as far as I'm concerned, as long as it's got fish, rice and eggs in it, you're home and dry.

# Ingredients

1 8oz. tin middle-cut
    salmon (or $\frac{3}{4}$ lb. piece
    cooked fresh salmon or
    smoked haddock)
4 ozs. button mushrooms
$\frac{1}{2}$ stock cube
Juice of half a lemon
6 ozs. rice
Salt and freshly ground
    pepper

1 small onion
1 pint milk
1 oz. plain flour
2 ozs. butter
Tip of a teaspoon curry
    powder
4 hard-boiled eggs
Fresh parsley
$\frac{1}{4}$ pint single cream
    (optional — see Method)

# Method

Boil the eggs for not more than 10 minutes from cold (they should still have a $\frac{1}{4}$ inch of soft centre). Run them under cold water until they are quite cold and then shell them. Cut them into quarters and then into eighths. Cover with foil until you require them.

Cook the rice in plenty of boiling light-salted water for 17 minutes exactly, then run it under the cold tap and wash off the starch. Leave to drain in a sieve or colander.

Finely slice the onion and mushrooms.

Melt the butter in a pan which will be large enough to contain all the ingredients. Add the sliced onions and fry until golden brown, then add the mushrooms and fry for a few seconds before stirring in the flour.

Add the touch of curry powder and the piece of stock cube. Gradually work in the cold milk a little at a time until you have a smooth sauce, and simmer for 5 minutes, stirring to ensure that it doesn't stick or burn.

If using tinned salmon, pour the juices from the tin into the sauce. Correct the seasoning and add lemon juice to acidulate lightly. Skin and flake the fish and fold into the sauce, then fold in the cooked rice and gently allow this to heat through, stirring with a 'folding' action as you do so, so that you do not break up the fish too much.

Finally, just before you are ready to serve the kedgeree,

carefully fold in the eggs. Pour the kedgeree into a heated dish, sprinkle with parsley and serve.

If the finished dish is too solid for you, add a $\frac{1}{4}$ pint of single cream brought to the boil.

I sometimes serve the rice separately, as it is possible to make it look more attractive this way, particularly if you mould the rice in a buttered ring-mould first, then fill the centre with the salmon (or haddock), eggs and mushrooms in their creamy sauce.

# Fricassée of Mushrooms

This isn't your wilted mushrooms slung into any old white sauce: I found this in my searches in an old cookbook — Patrick Lamb, Queen Anne's cook, no less; my friend Escoffier didn't half prick up his little French ears when I showed it to him. (Mind you, I didn't tell him that Patrick Lamb had had a stint in France and might well have picked it up over there!)

## Ingredients

| | |
|---|---|
| 8 ozs. button mushrooms | Juice of half a lemon |
| $\frac{1}{4}$ pint double cream | 2 egg-yolks |
| Salt and cayenne pepper | |

## Method

Wipe the mushrooms clean of all dirt, but do not wash them. Slice them finely, squeeze the lemon juice over, season lightly and place in a pan over very low heat.

Toss the mushrooms until they 'draw' and their juices become sufficient for them to cook. Take care not to over-cook them or they will become like pieces of leather. Pour over them all but a tablespoon of the cream. Bring to the boil.

Mix the last tablespoon of cream with the egg-yolks and stir this briskly into the sauce, but *do not* re-boil. Check the seasoning.

65

# Creamed Veal Kidneys

You must use calves' or veal kidneys, which are soft and tender as a baby's bottom, for this recipe. No good hoping old ox kidney will do, because it won't — only the best ingredients when you're using cream and wine.

## Ingredients

6 calves' or veal kidneys
2 ozs. butter
$\frac{1}{4}$ pint double cream
$\frac{1}{4}$ teaspoon powdered
   rosemary or ginger

4 ozs. button mushrooms
2 tablespoons Madeira or
   medium dry sherry
Salt and freshly ground
   pepper

## Method

Skin and trim the kidneys of all fat; slice them thinly. Wash and slice the mushrooms.

Melt the butter in a frying pan until it foams and fry the kidneys until they are tender (if your pan is not very large, it is better to do this in two batches). Season the kidneys lightly with rosemary or ginger, salt and pepper and remove them to a warm serving dish. Toss the mushrooms in pan juices, adding more butter if necessary. Pour over Madeira and cream, cook until sauce has cohered like thick cream. Pour over kidneys, reheat and serve.

# Kippers with Marmalade

Lord Henry Norton brought this recipe back with him from his Scottish shooting lodge near Braemar. It's a great favourite at the Bentinck — once you've got over the unusual idea you'll like it as well.

# Method

Brush the kippers with melted butter and grill them gently for from 5 to 8 minutes. Heat 2 tablespoons of dark marmalade and press this through a fine sieve. Add a squeeze of lemon juice and spoon a trickle down the middle of each grilled kipper.

Dredge a tiny bit of nutmeg over and serve them as hot as a jockey's breeches!

---

# The Savoury

No Edwardian menu is complete without that British institution — *The Savoury*.

As far as I'm concerned, it beats the French with their cheese; not that I'm against cheese, mind, but I'm not too sure that *we* aren't right in having it at the end of a meal (not after the main dish like they do). Certainly at a luncheon I'd leave it in this place on an English menu, and I don't hardly ever serve cheese at a dinner, except it's a good Stilton served together with green walnuts and a glass of Offley or Forrester, a Warre or Fonsecca, and an 1870 at that.

Nothing the French have thought up can replace this good English tradition: because it's more than eating and drinking — it's a ceremony.

And I'm going to raise my little Duke Street voice again and ask you to throw out those cheese scoops, or spoons, or whatever you choose to call them. Disaster they are. Never did a Stilton any good, they only ruin it! Digging in the middle like a sexton in a graveyard, it's not logical.

Take a good knife and cut 'V'-shaped wedges *across* the cheese. This way everybody gets a bit of ripe and a fair proportion of the rest. Keep your cheese covered with a buttered paper, under a Stilton dome and it'll keep in good condition for weeks instead of falling apart like Cromwell's ruins. I'll not be popular with some of my friends in the hotel trade for saying this, but I feel it's right to speak my mind on the subject.

Many people eschew sweets either from questions of taste or of health or because food of a saccharine nature leads to obesity. So the savoury slots in nicely in lieu of or in addition to a sweet. They can be hot or cold, and can be little soufflés, ramekins, canapés or beignets. I like to send up a large soufflé in a silver liner to each 'salon privé'.

---

# Cheese Beignets

---

These take a bit of practice to make — not that they're difficult, it's just that if your fat's too hot, a crust forms and they can't swell up like they should. If your fat's too cool, then they get soggy.

So practise with a bit of the mixture 'til you get it right. (Temperature should be approx. 325°F.)

You can make them almost of anything — mushroom purée, spinach, ham and so on. But for a savoury, I think cheese is the best.

## Ingredients

*Choux pastry:*
⅜ pint water
3¾ ozs. flour

3 ozs. butter
3 eggs (small)

(Make up as on p. 194)

2 ozs. finely grated
  Parmesan cheese
Salt and pepper

½ teaspoon made English
  mustard
More grated Parmesan
  for dredging

# Method

Mix the grated cheese and seasoning into the choux paste. Lightly oil some kitchen paper. Scoop rounded spoonsful onto the oiled paper. Dip a palette knife into hot fat and lift up the prepared spoonsful, sliding them gently into the fryer — not too many at a time as they need room to swell.

Cook for about 8 minutes when they will be 'floating', golden, and crisp.

Drain well on crumpled paper.

Arrange on a crisp white serviette: dredge with Parmesan and a modicum of paprika, black pepper, or better still, grated nutmeg.

---

# Louisa Trotter's Cheese Straws

## Ingredients

5 ozs. plain flour
4 ozs. unsalted butter
2 egg yolks
2 ozs. freshly grated
   Parmesan cheese

Good pinch of salt —
  $\frac{1}{4}$ teaspoon
Pinch cayenne pepper
  (optional)
1 teaspoon lemon juice

1 tablespoon cold water

## Method

Mix yolks, lemon juice and water together. Rub fat into flour until sand-like texture is arrived at. Toss in grated Parmesan cheese. Season lightly, tossing well in. Make well, pour in the liquids, mix quickly and form deftly into a paste. Leave for 1 hour in a cold place.

Roll out into one sheet of $\frac{1}{4}$ inch thick, cut into 2 inch wide strips. Place these onto a buttered baking sheet, mark out the strips into $\frac{1}{4}$ to $\frac{1}{2}$ inch sticks.

Dredge with further grated Parmesan if the budget permits! Bake (at Gas 6, Electric 400°) for 7 to 8 minutes, or until crisp and golden brown.

Remove with the aid of a palette knife to a cooling tray. Divide when quite cool. Store in airtight tin.

# Angels on Horseback

Cut oval bread shapes no more than 2 inches long and $\frac{1}{3}$ inch thick. Toast these delicately, spread with lemon-flavoured butter, and top with a juicy oyster wrapped round with a sliver of streaky bacon and quickly grilled.

# Devils on Horseback

Make toasts as in Angels on Horseback. Before buttering them with unflavoured butter, spread a modicum of made English mustard on the toasts. (This is different to mixing the mustard with the butter). Top with a pitted cooked prune which has been stuffed with hot chutney, wrapped with bacon and grilled.

# Scotch Woodcock

For a change we used to butter-fry the croûtons for this savoury. Make scrambled eggs (p.61). Pile the finished eggs onto the croûtons. Place 2 anchovy fillets diagonally across the eggs, leaving a narrow channel. Fill this with finely chopped capers and sprinkle with a little freshly chopped parsley.

# Derby Toasts

Make round toasts from brown bread. Spread with a little made mustard, then butter fairly lightly and spread with a mixture of:
  Minced lean cooked ham
  Thick cream to bind to a spreadable paste
  Egg yolk (1 to 4 ozs ham)
  Salt and pepper
  Pinch of mustard
Top with half a pickled walnut, and brown under a hot grill.

# Sardines on Toast

Now this little savoury can be good, or the sardines can look about as interesting as dead men on a coffin lid.

Mrs Cochrane and me thought this one up for Lord Henry (Norton), him liking fish so much, and forever dining at the Bentinck.

## Method

Make oval shapes from brown bread (remember keep them thin, ⅓ inch, no more). Either fry these in good butter, or spread them with lemon-flavoured butter (put a little bit of finely grated rind in this time). Now spread with this mixture:

71

| 4 ozs. mashed sardines | 1 teaspoon mild-flavoured |
| 1 teaspoon onion juice |    mustard |
| 1 teaspoon lemon juice | A touch of salt if needed |

Skin and fillet half a sardine for the top of each toast. Heat through under the grill and pour just a drop of melted butter over each one before serving, sprinkled with plenty of chopped parsley and chives.

# Soups
# & Sauces

## The Lord Mayor's Soup

When H.M. gave a big luncheon at The Guildhall in Bangor for the Prince of Wales (later George V), I got asked to do it.

We took the whole bleedin' lot up from London, we did. Planned like a military operation it was. Because there weren't any kitchens at The Guildhall everything was cold except for the soup; and it was this original old Mansion House recipe we used.

We prefer to have this soup made, in part, the evening before it is wanted. *An Agnes Marshall recipe.*

### Ingredients

| | |
|---|---|
| 8 moderate-sized pigs' feet | 4 pigs' ears |
| 5 quarts water | 1 tablespoonful salt |
| 2 onions | 1 head of celery |

| | |
|---|---|
| 2 carrots | Bunch of herbs |
| 1 small teaspoonful peppercorns | 1 blade mace |

Cook for 3½ to 4½ hours

| | |
|---|---|
| 5 pints stock | 6 ozs. rice flour |
| ¼ teaspoonful cayenne | ¾ teaspoonful each mace and salt |
| Juice of one lemon | |
| 3 tablespoonsful Harvey's sauce | ½ pint sherry or Madeira |

Cook for 6 to 8 minutes

| | |
|---|---|
| 2 tablespoonsful savoury · herbs | |

Cook for a further 5 minutes

Observation: should the quantity of stock exceed 5 pints, an additional ounce or more of rice must be used, and the flavouring be altogether increased in proportion. Of the minced herbs, two-thirds should be parsley, and the remainder equal parts of lemon thyme and winter savoury, unless sweet basil should be at hand, when a teaspoonful of it may be substituted for half of the parsley.

To some tastes a seasoning of sage would be acceptable; and a slice or two of lean ham will much improve the flavour of the soup.

## Method

Wash thoroughly two sets of moderate sized pigs' ears and feet from which the hair has been carefully removed; add to them 5 quarts of cold water. Skim it thoroughly when it first boils, and throw in a tablespoonful of salt, two onions of moderate size, a small head of celery, a bunch of herbs, two whole carrots, a small teaspoonful of white peppercorns, and a blade of mace.

Stew these softly until the ears and feet are perfectly tender, and, after they are lifted out, let the liquor be kept *just simmering* only, while they are being boned, that it may not be too much reduced. Put the bones back into it, and stew them as gently as possible for an hour; then strain the soup into a clean pan, and set it by until the morrow in a cool place.

The flesh should be cut into dice while it is still warm, and covered with the cloth before it becomes *quite* cold.

To prepare the soup for table, clear the stock from fat and sediment, put it into a very clean stewpan, or deep saucepan, and stir into it when it boils 6 ozs. of the finest rice-flour smoothly mixed with ¼ teaspoonful of cayenne, three times as much of mace and salt, the strained juice of a lemon, 3 tablespoonsful of Harvey's sauce, and ½ pint of good sherry or Madeira. Simmer the whole for 6 or 8 minutes, add more salt if needed, stir the soup often, and skim it thoroughly; put in the meat and herbs, and after they have boiled gently for 5 minutes, dish the soup, add forcemeat-balls or not, at pleasure, and send it to table quickly.

# Oyster Soup

## Ingredients

2 doz. oysters (frozen will suffice)
4 ozs. unsalted butter
2 ozs. flour
½ pint single cream
2 egg-yolks
Cayenne pepper

2-pints fish stock (made with bones from about 6 soles stewed for half-an-hour in water only)
Juice of half a lemon or a small glass of white Burgundy

Salt and freshly ground white pepper

## Method

Melt the butter in a heavy-bottomed pan, but do not let it get hot. Stir in the flour. Add the strained fish stock and bring this to the boil, stirring all the time.

Add the cream (reserving a little to mix with the egg-yolks) and the juice from the oysters if they are fresh ones. Adjust the seasoning, and gradually add the lemon juice or wine to your taste. Bring to the boil and strain.

Add the oysters just before you are ready to serve the soup —

no sooner or they will toughen.

At the last minute, when the soup is in the tureen, mix the egg-yolks with the reserved cream and stir briskly into the hot soup. Sprinkle just a dash of cayenne pepper on the surface of the soup before serving.

# Louisa Trotter's Oxtail Broth

## Ingredients

2 lbs. oxtail pieces
Oil for frying
½ pint red wine
Glass of Madeira or sherry
1 medium onion
1 large leek
½ oz. flour per pint of
    finished soup
1 oz. butter
*Garnish:* butter-fried croûtons

Cold water
1½ pints stock (made half
    strength from stock cube)
Stick of celery
2 carrots
Mustard-spoon each of:
    powdered basil, mace,
    thyme, marjoram
Salt and freshly milled black
    pepper

1 tablespoon freshly chopped parsley

## Method

Have your butcher chop the oxtail into smallish pieces. Put these into a pan with enough cold water to cover. Bring to the boil, simmer for 5 minutes. Pour away the water. Pat pieces of oxtail dry with kitchen paper. Have ready a 4 pint pan or oven pot. Heat the oil in a heavy-bottomed frying pan, and brown the pieces of oxtail on all sides — this is a messy job if done properly, as a high heat is required; the pieces should be done a few at a time so that the temperature is not reduced too greatly.

Transfer these to your pot. Clean and cut the vegetables into pieces. In the same frying pan, let these acquire a good golden colour. Transfer them to the pot with the oxtail. Cover with the wine and stock (not the Madeira). Add the spices and simmer the whole lot for 3 hours in a low oven or on top of the stove.

Now strain the soup into a clean pan. Discard the vegetables which will be more or less pulp. Bring the strained soup to the boil, and whisk in a blend of the flour and butter in the proportions mentioned. Season delicately. A touch of natural brown colouring is permissible in this recipe, if the colour of the soup is not deep enough.

Pick the meat from the pieces of oxtail, chop these roughly, and add to the soup together with the Madeira or sherry and freshly chopped parsley just before serving.

Serve the croûtons separately.

# Mulligatawny Soup

## Ingredients

| | |
|---|---|
| 2 quarts water | 2 lbs. mutton |
| 2 onions | 2 carrots |
| 2 apples | 1 small turnip |
| A bouquet-garni (parsley, | 2 tablespoonsful of flour |
| thyme, bay-leaf) | 1 tablespoonful of curry |
| Juice of half a lemon | powder |
| Salt | |

## Method

Remove the fat from the mutton and melt it in the saucepan. Have the apples and vegetables ready sliced, and when there is sufficient liquid fat to fry them, take out the pieces of fat, put in the vegetables, and cook them for 15 minutes. Sprinkle in the flour and curry powder, fry for a few minutes, then add the meat in small pieces, a teaspoonful of salt, the herbs and water. When the compound boils, remove the scum as it rises, then cover and cook gently for 3 hours. Strain, rub the meat through a wire sieve, and return to the saucepan. When boiling, add the lemon juice, season to taste, and serve. Well-cooked rice should be handed round with this soup.

# Tomato, Orange and Prawn Soup

## Ingredients

1½ pints tomato juice (fresh or tinned)
1 pint fish stock
¾ lb prawns *in shells* (use frozen ones)
4 ozs. butter
Salt and pepper
*Garnish* 2 oranges
Shelled prawns (see ingredients)
6 tomatoes

¾ pint orange juice (use tinned or frozen)
½ bottle dry white wine
2 medium onions
4 cloves garlic
2 ozs. flour
½ pint cream
2 doz. baby quenelles (see below)
2 tablespoons chopped parsley

## Method

Melt butter, finely chop onion, crush the garlic. Sweat (soften) onions until tender. Add garlic. Stir in flour, gradually add all liquids except cream. Add prawn *shells* only. Simmer for 30 minutes.

Whilst soup is simmering, segment the oranges ensuring there is no pith on the segments. Make the baby quenelles (see below). Skin, deseed and concassée (chop) the tomatoes. Chop the parsley. Strain the soup. Add the cream. Check seasoning; add the concasséed tomato, quenelles and prawns; re-heat *but do not allow to boil.* Pour the soup into individual dishes: add orange segments, sprinkle with parsley and serve.

*Baby Quenelles:* Make up a pint of savoury choux paste. Fill into a (savoy) piping bag fitted with a ¼ inch plain tube. Have a shallow pan of salted water simmering; 'sit' the nozzle of the bag on the rim of the pan, *gently* press the mixture out, and, as it drops into the water, 'cut' it off at ½ inch intervals with a wetted knife. Poach the quenelles for 10 minutes or so; lift out as they are cooked, with a draining spoon, and put into cold water until required. Re-heat in hot water; drain well before adding to the soup.

# Turnip Soup

## Ingredients

| | |
|---|---|
| 1½ lbs. turnip (peeled weight) | 2 ozs. butter |
| 2 pints veal or chicken stock | 2 ozs. dry (but not stale) brown bread |
| 2 ozs. onion | 1 tablespoon olive oil |
| ½ level teaspoon nutmeg | Large glass of medium dry |
| Watercress to garnish | sherry or Madeira |

Salt and freshly ground black pepper

## Method

Chop the onion, peel and cut the turnip into 1 inch cubes. Melt the butter in a heavy-bottomed pan, swirling it round until it is foaming and giving off a delicious 'nutty' flavour. Add the onions and the turnip. Cover with a lid and 'sweat' the vegetables gently over a low heat until they are tender. This will take about 25 minutes.

Cut the brown bread, crusts and all, into ½ inch cubes. In a separate frying pan, heat the olive oil and fry the bread cubes until crisp and evenly browned — move them about constantly to achieve this even colouring.

Add the fried bread to the turnip. Add the sherry and the cold stock, and cook gently for a further 20 minutes.

Season with the salt, pepper and nutmeg. Pass through a blender or Mouli.

Serve with sprigs of watercress on a side plate.

# Pea Soup

I don't think the French have the right idea about pea soup.

Try this recipe what we've developed from an old eighteenth century English recipe.

## Ingredients

4 ozs. (frozen) peas
1 small rasher bacon
3 ozs. onion
1 scant ounce plain flour
Half a lettuce

1½ pints chicken stock
1 oz. butter
2 small sticks celery
½ teaspoon fresh rosemary
  leaves

*For the Bentinck garnish*
4 rashers good-flavoured
  green bacon
Enough fresh mint leaves to
  cover these rashers

Minuscule triangular croûtons
  (white bread fried in butter),
  not more than ½ inch
  wide at base

## Method

Slice the onions and chop the celery, shred the lettuce and cut the first bacon rasher into thin strips.

In one pan bring to the boil the cold stock and frozen peas. Simmer for a few minutes until the peas are just tender.

In a second pan melt the butter and fry the onions and bacon until pale golden colour. Add the celery, cover with a lid and 'sweat' until soft. Stir in the flour and add the rosemary leaves.

Bring the contents of the two pans together and add the shredded lettuce. Simmer for 10 minutes. Pass through a Mouli or blender — as a coarse-textured soup is preferable, the former is recommended. If you use a blender, take care to ensure that the soup is not over-puréed.

Make the bacon rolls, which must be minuscule, de-rind each rasher and 'spread' the meat out with the wetted flat of a knife. Lay mint leaves to cover completely the surface of the rasher and roll up tightly. Secure with a cocktail stick and fry gently until you are sure the bacon is cooked inside. Remove the sticks and cut each roll into $\frac{1}{8}$ inch pieces. This garnish is an integral part of the soup and ugly or clumsy preparation at this stage will spoil an otherwise delectable start to a meal.

Re-heat soup, check seasoning and add croûtons and bacon rolls to each bowl *just* before serving.

# Danish Cauliflower Soup

We don't think in our kitchens that the French Crème Dubarry is all that interesting. Try our way of making cauliflower soup. The Queen (Alexandra) liked this recipe because it's similar to how they make it in Denmark where she hails from.

## Ingredients

| | |
|---|---|
| 1 medium-sized very white and firm cauliflower | 1 pint chicken stock |
| 1 oz. plain flour | 1 pint milk |
| Grated nutmeg | 2 ozs. butter |
| A touch of yellow colouring | One poached or lightly boiled egg per person |

Salt

# Method

Divide the cauliflower into finger-tip-sized florets. Patience at this stage will be very rewarding.

Bring the stock to the boil. Drop in the florets and poach gently for *7 minutes,* no longer, for the secret of this soup is to have the florets cooked but *firm.* With a wire strainer, lift out the florets and place on one side. Add the milk to the stock and bring to boiling point.

In a second small pan, melt the butter, stir in the flour and blend well. Whisk this mixture into the now gently boiling milk and stock. Simmer the soup over a low heat for 5 minutes.

Season with salt and a little grated nutmeg, about the tip of a teaspoon at first. Add more if you like the combination. Now add the merest touch of yellow colouring (known in the trade as 'egg yellow'). You are not aiming at a canary yellow — just a creamy colour. This is a technique to be encouraged, but take care not to use lemon colouring as this often has a synthetic flavour with it.

Strain the soup into a clean pan, add the florets and re-heat carefully.

# Sauces

If I was writing a big cookery book, I'd have a lot to say in this section, but this book's just to help you entertain better. It's enough here to say that sauces are divided up like this:

*Basic Sauces* the French call them *Sauces Mères* — 'Mother' sauces.

i   Brown Sauce *(Sauces Brunes)*
ii  White Sauces *(Sauces Blanches)* (Velouté Sauce comes into this little lot)
iii Butter Sauces *(Sauces au Beurre)*
iv  Cold Sauces (I put both brown and white chaudfroid sauces

into this part)

v Miscellaneous Sauces (tomato, horseradish, mint, apple etc.)

vi Sweet Sauces (fruit, jam, custards, caramels, sweet butters)

The basic ways of thickening sauces are as follows:

i White or brown roux

ii *Beurre Manié* (Rolled Butter, we called this method in the 18th century)

iii Slaked flour; cornflour; arrowroot; or potato flour

iv With egg yolks (and cream)

v With beaten butter

vi With blood

# Escoffier on Brown Sauce

My French friend came to the Bentinck one day and after a glass or two of the old bubbly I got him talking about wine sauces — me not holding all that much with wine cookery and him trying to convince me like.

'Louise, ma chère femme, je vais te montrer moi-même!' Bless his little French heart; right into our kitchen he went. My girls was thrilled to bits. Fair took them aback when the *King* of cooks tied an apron round his big middle and started to rattle away in French — me translating as he went along if you please! I got him back a time or two when we had 'French' problems. I like to think he used a few of my good English recipes; well, I knew he did, both at the Carlton and the Savoy. I saw me own touch in the steak puddings and he created his own version of my Quail Pudding, though I reckon he got a bit too fancy with that; mine's better. You can *taste* the quail and that's what it's all about. Anyway, here's what he taught us all about brown sauces.

# Brown Sauce or Espagnole

*Quantities Required for Four Quarts:* One lb. of brown roux dissolved in a tall, thick saucepan with six quarts of brown stock or estouffade. Put the saucepan on an open fire, and stir the sauce with a spatula or a whisk, and do not leave it until it begins to boil. Then remove the spatula, and put the saucepan on a corner of the fire, letting it lean slightly to one side with the help of a wedge, so that boiling may only take place at one point, and that the inert principles thrown out by the sauce during despumation may accumulate high up in the saucepan, whence they can be easily removed as they collect.

It is advisable during despumation to change saucepans twice or even three times, straining every time, and adding a quart of brown stock to replace what has evaporated. At length, when the sauce begins to get lighter, and about two hours before finally straining it, 2 lbs. fresh tomatoes, roughly cut up, should be added, or an equivalent quantity of tomato purée, and about 1 lb. of mirepoix. The sauce is then reduced so as to measure 4 quarts when strained, after which it is poured into a wide tureen, and must be kept in motion until quite cool lest a skin should form on its surface.

The time required for the despumation of an Espagnole varies according to the quality of the stock and roux. We saw above that one hour sufficed for a concentrated stock and starch roux, in which case the mirepoix and the tomato are inserted from the first. But much more time is required if one is dealing with a roux whose base is flour. In the latter case six hours should be allowed, provided one has excellent stock and well-made roux. More often than not this work is done in two stages, thus: after having despumated the Espagnole for six or eight hours the first day, it is put on the fire the next day with half its volume of stock, and it is left to despumate a few hours more before it is finally strained.

Summing up my opinion on this subject, I can only give my colleagues the following advice, based upon long experience. Firstly, only use strong, clear stock with a decided taste. Secondly, be scrupulously careful of the roux, however it may be made. By following these two rules, a clear, brilliant, and consistent Espagnole will always be obtained in a fairly short time.

# Half Glaze (Demi-Glace)

This is the Espagnole sauce, having reached the limit of perfection by final despumation. It is obtained by reducing one quart of Espagnole and one quart of first-class brown stock until its volume is reduced to nine-tenths of a quart. It is then strained into a *bain-marie* of convenient dimensions, and it is finished, away from the fire, with one-tenth of a quart of excellent sherry.

Cover the *bain-marie,* or slightly butter the top to avoid the formation of a skin. This sauce is the base of all the smaller brown sauces.

# Madeira Sauce

To half a pint of demi-glace, add 2 tablespoons of medium dry Madeira.

# Lyonnaise Sauce

Fry 1 oz. of finely sliced onions in $\frac{1}{2}$ oz. of butter until quite brown. Add 2 tablespoons of dry white wine and 2 teaspoons wine vinegar. Boil rapidly until viscous. Add half a pint of demi-glace (p.85). Simmer for a further 15 minutes.

# Remarks on Red Wine Sauces

In the general repertory of cooking, we also have, in the way of red wine sauces, the *Bourguignonne, Matelote,* and 'Red Wine' sauces, which are closely allied to the *Genevoise,* and only differ from it in details of procedure.

The *Bourguignonne* Sauce is composed of red wine accompanied by aromatics, and reduced by half. In accordance with ordinary principles, it is thickened by means of 3 ozs. of maniéd butter per quart of reduced wine. This sauce is buttered with 4 ozs. of butter per quart, and is especially regarded as a domestic preparation for poached, moulded, and hard-boiled eggs.

*Matelote* Sauce is made from court-bouillon, with red wine which has been used for cooking fish. This court-bouillon, with the mushroom parings added, is reduced by two-thirds, and is thickened with one pint of Lenten Espagnole per pint of the reduced court-bouillon.

This sauce should be reduced by a third, strained through a tammy, and finished by means of 2 ozs. of butter and a little cayenne per pint of sauce.

The Red Wine Sauce resembles the two preceding ones in so far as it contains mirepoix browned in butter and diluted with red wine. The wine is reduced by half, thickened by a pint of Lenten Espagnole per pint of the reduction, and the sauce is despumated for about 20 minutes. It is strained through a tammy, and finished, when ready, by a few drops of anchovy essence, a little cayenne, and 2 ozs. of butter per pint of sauce.

# Sauce Bordelaise

Put into a vegetable pan 2 ozs. of very finely minced shallots, one half pint of good red wine, a pinch of pepper, and bits of thyme and bay. Reduce the wine by three-quarters, and add one half pint of demi-glace. Keep the sauce simmering for half an hour; despumate it from time to time, and strain it through linen or a sieve.

When dishing it up, finish it with two tablespoonsful of dissolved meat glaze (half a meat stock cube), a few drops of lemon juice, and 4 ozs. beef-marrow, cut into slices or cubes and poached in slightly salted boiling water. This sauce may be buttered to the extent of about 3 ozs. per pint, which makes it smoother, but less clear. It is especially suitable for grilled butchers' meat.

# White Chaudfroid Sauce

1 oz. butter
$\frac{3}{4}$ pint milk
$\frac{1}{4}$ pint made aspic jelly
$\frac{1}{4}$ pint cream
Lemon juice

1 oz. flour
Dessertspoon gelatine
  (crystals)
Salt and *white* pepper (black
  pepper leaves specks)

## Method

Make up a white sauce from the butter, flour and milk. Dissolve gelatine in the warm aspic; add to the white sauce. Stir in the cream, season interestingly adding lemon juice to taste. Strain through fine sieve and/or linen cloth.

Arrange bowl over ice and water, stirring until as thick as thick cream. Then coat the waiting *chilled* foods.

# Brown Chaudfroid Sauce

## Ingredients

¾ pint demi-glace sauce
 (p.85)
¼ pint dry Madeira

¾ pint made aspic jelly
 Dessertspoon gelatine
 (crystals)

## Method

Warm the demi-glace sauce. Warm aspic, dissolve gelatine in this. Add to demi-glace, together with Madeira.

Follow on as for white chaudfroid sauce, coating foods when consistency is right.

# Tomata Sauce

*An Eliza Acton recipe* Tomatas are so juicy when ripe that they require little or no liquid to reduce them to a proper consistency for sauce; and they vary so exceedingly in size and quality that it is difficult to give precise directions for the exact quantity which in their unripe state is needed for them. Take off the stalks, halve the tomatas, and gently squeeze out the seeds and watery pulp; then stew them softly with a few spoonsful of gravy or of strong broth until they are quite melted. Press the whole through a hair-sieve, and heat it afresh with a little additional gravy should it be too thick, and some cayenne, and salt. Serve it very hot.

Fine ripe tomatas, 6 or 8; gravy or strong broth, 4 tablespoonsful; ½ to ¾ hour, or longer if needed. Salt and cayenne sufficient to season the sauce, and two or three spoonsful more of gravy if required.

*Obs* For a large tureen of this sauce, increase the proportions; and should it be at first too liquid, reduce it by quick boiling. When neither gravy nor broth is at hand, the tomatas may be stewed perfectly tender, but very gently, in a couple of ounces of butter, with some cayenne and salt only, or with the addition of a very little finely minced onion; then rubbed through a sieve, and heated, and served without any additon, or with only that of a teaspoonful of chili vinegar; or, when the colour is not a principal consideration, with a few spoonsful of rich cream, smoothly mixed with a little flour to prevent its curdling. The sauce must be stirred without ceasing should the last be added, and boiled for four to five minutes.

(Miss Acton's recipe in her 'Observation' is better than the original — particularly when cream is added.)

# Béchamel

*An Eliza Acton recipe* This is a fine French white sauce, now very much served at good English tables. It may be made in various ways, and more or less expensively; but it should always be thick, smooth, and rich, though delicate in flavour. The most ready mode of preparing it is to take an equal portion of very strong, pale veal gravy, and of good cream (a pint of each for example), and then, by rapid boiling over a very clear fire, to reduce the gravy nearly half; next, to mix with part of the cream a tablespoonful of fine dry flour, to pour it to the remainder, when it boils, and to keep the whole stirred for five minutes or more over a slow fire, for if placed upon a fierce one it would be liable to burn; then to add the gravy, to stir and mix the sauce perfectly, and to simmer it for a few minutes longer. All the flavour should be given by the gravy, in which French cooks boil a handful of mushrooms, a *few* green onions, and some branches of parsley before it is reduced: but a good *béchamel* may be made without them, with a strong *consommé* well reduced.

Strong pale veal gravy (flavoured with mushrooms or not); 1 pint: reduced half. Rich cream, 1 pint; flour, 1 tablespoonful: 5 minutes. With gravy, 4 or 5 minutes.

I like Miss Acton's instructions for this French classic sauce, but there is an easier and better way to make it.

# Béchamel II

## Ingredients

¾ pint veal stock      ¾ pint thin cream
2 ozs. butter      1½ ozs. flour
Salt, pepper, lemon juice

## Method

Reduce stock and cream to one pint. Melt butter in a second pan, stir in flour; gradually incorporate reduction stirring well. Reduce heat and simmer for 15 minutes. Season with salt, pepper and lemon juice. Strain through a fine sieve.

# Allemande Sauce

I started using Bertha's (Agnes B. Marshall) recipe for this sauce, and can see not much of a better way as yet.

Put 2½ ozs. of butter into a stewpan with 2½ ozs. of fine flour, and fry together without discolouring: then mix it with 1½ pints of good-flavoured white stock, either from veal, rabbit, or chicken. Stir till it boils, then add ¼ pint of washed fresh white mushrooms that have been cut in thin slices, boil for about 15 minutes, then stir in 4 raw yolks of eggs that have been mixed with a gill of thick cream, a dust of coralline pepper (paprika), and the juice of half a lemon. Stir the sauce over the fire again until it thickens, then have it rubbed through a clean tammy cloth and use.

# Mushroom Sauce

To each pint of Allemande Sauce (p.90) add 8 ozs. finely sliced white mushrooms 'softened' in 1 oz. of butter. (When required for use with fish, make up the Allemande Sauce with fish stock).

# Périgueux Sauce

To half a pint of Madeira Sauce, add 1 oz. very finely chopped truffles, and a little truffle juice from the tin.

# Bread Sauce

## Ingredients

½ pint milk
1 small onion, roughly
  chopped
Salt and freshly ground
  white pepper
¼ pint single cream

2 ozs. butter
Half crushed clove garlic
One bay leaf (or a little
  nutmeg or 2 cloves)
3 ozs. fresh white bread-
  crumbs

A little white stock or extra milk

## Method

Put the milk, butter, garlic, bay leaf or nutmeg or cloves, and onion into the top of a double saucepan and make the mixture as hot as possible. Add the breadcrumbs and let the sauce cook until it is quite thick and smooth. Pass the entire contents of the pan through a fine sieve (blender, Mouli).

Add the cream, adjust the seasoning, re-heat and serve.

If the sauce is too thick (this will depend on the kind of bread you use) let it down with a little white stock, cream or milk.

*Note* If the sauce has to be kept hot, return it to the double saucepan after sieving, and cover with a circle of buttered paper to prevent a skin forming. Keep the water in the bottom pan hot.

# Apple Sauce

## Ingredients

4 Cox's Orange Pippins          1 tablespoon castor sugar
About 1 oz. unsalted butter

# Method

Peel, quarter and core the apples, Cut into even-sized slices and poach in a modicum of water, plus 1 oz. of unsalted butter per pound of apples, until tender.

Add the sugar and stir well until dissolved. Pass through a fine sieve (blender or Mouli) and chill well. This recipe will give you a rich firm sauce.

# Mayonnaise

Mrs Wellkin always had bother with her mayonnaise. Split like a pig's ear it used to be. She never got it thick and creamy. Do you know why? She didn't understand that she was making an *emulsion*. Oil and water beat up hard makes an emulsion, but it'll separate out if you don't 'stabilise' it with egg yolks.

Then you've got to add your oil *slow,* so that the yolks can assimilate it. An egg yolk can take about 2 fluid ounces of oil, depending on its size and, of course, the quality of the oil — better oil's better at it — and you've got to beat hard (or use a machine).

Then you've got to have your oil at room temperature. Then, get your salt in *early:* this helps your yolks to thicken.

So, here's the major points what I tell them to remember in the bowels of the old Bentinck:

i   Don't add your oil too quick: start with a drop at a time — and I mean a drop.

ii  Don't use cold oil (straight from the pantry).

iii Work out how much oil you'll need to each yolk, and don't add *no more* than what you need.

iv  If you want a pale mayonnaise, use lemon instead of vinegar.

v   Use a round-bottomed basin *small enough to control* the quantity you're making. If it does split — and it shouldn't if

'Salvaging Mrs Wellkin's split mayonnaise.'

you do like I say — Beat up 2 egg yolks with a pinch of salt 'til they're thick, then add your curdled mayonnaise — drop by drop — finish it off with a tablespoon of boiling water.

## Ingredients

12 fluid ounces oil (half
   nut-oil, half good olive
   oil) at room temperature
Cold water

6 egg yolks
1 teaspoon dry mustard
1 tablespoon wine vinegar
Salt and freshly ground
   white pepper

## Method

Separate the eggs and put the yolks into a round-bottomed basin. This is an essential as you need to 'collect' and control the yolks within a small area. Add the salt, mustard and a little pepper, and work these with a balloon whisk, or more laboriously with a wooden spoon, until they are really thick and 'sticky'.

Have the oil in a jug; then, using a teaspoon, add the first few drops of oil to the egg mixture, whisking vigorously. Beat this well in before adding the next few drops. It is essential to take care in the *early* stages of mayonnaise making — if you are meticulous at the beginning, you will have no trouble later.

After the first tablespoonful or so has been added slowly, you can start to add the oil more quickly — experience will teach you just when this can be done. As soon as the emulsion starts to reject the oil (this is quite different from curdling) add a little vinegar or cold water and beat until it is creamy again. Mayonnaise is curdled when the solid part goes thin and flecky. If this happens, you must start again with a single egg yolk and work the curdled mayonnaise into it drop by drop. *Sometimes* a tablespoon of boiling water added to the curdled mayonnaise will do the trick.

Keep the mayonnaise as stiff as your arm will allow ! By this

I mean that if you have a strong arm you will be able to have mayonnaise as thick as butter, which can virtually be cut with a knife. When a more liquid mayonnaise is needed, thin down with single cream, vinegar or cold water (or a combination of all three); water gives a blander result than vinegar, cream adds richness.

The finished mayonnaise can be flavoured with ketchup, sherry, lemon juice, brandy, Worcester sauce, etc.

When next using mayonnaise to make tartar sauce, try adding a few chopped raw gooseberries — this will give a delicious 'kick' to the sauce.

Store mayonnaise in a cool, but not cold, place. It does not keep indefinitely, but will be quite all right for 4 or 5 days. If it begins to look oily, just add a spoonful of boiling water and whisk until it is creamy again. You can't beat a good French mayonnaise for most things, but the old-fashioned English boiled salad creams and dressings make cold meats and salads a deal more interesting — especially salmon and cold boiled capon. And what's more, they're as English as me.

These two recipes are from Yorkshire families I've met since I knew Charlie Haslemere. They're both worth a try.

# Salad Dressing

## Ingredients

| | |
|---|---|
| 1 dessertspoon mustard | 2 eggs |
| ½ teaspoon salt | 1 good tablespoon sugar |
| Pinch of cayenne pepper | ½ teacup of milk |
| 1 oz. butter | ½ breakfastcup vinegar |

## Method

Mix dry ingredients to a paste with milk. Beat the eggs and mix in. Add the vinegar *slowly*. Put in a double cooker and cook until it begins to thicken.

Take off heat and add the butter. When cold bottle and keep well-stoppered.

# Boiled Salad Cream

## Ingredients

| | |
|---|---|
| 1 tablespoon flour | 1 teaspoon salt |
| $\frac{1}{2}$ teaspoon pepper | 4 teaspoons mustard |
| 1 egg | 4 ozs. sugar |
| 4 teaspoons salad oil | 1 pint milk |

$\frac{1}{2}$ pint white vinegar *or* $\frac{1}{4}$ pint brown vinegar

## Method

Mix all dry ingredients together, add oil and sugar. Beat the egg well into the milk, and then gradually mix with the dry ingredients. Add vinegar slowly, and then thicken in a double boiler. Bottle when cold.

# Green Sauce

To each $\frac{1}{2}$ pint basic mayonnaise, add $\frac{1}{2}$ oz. each of parsley, chives, tarragon, chervil, sorrel-leaves, all finely chopped, and 1 oz. of watercress, and 1 oz. of spinach leaves. Boil in lightly salted water for 2 minutes — no longer — drain, run under cold water, drain well again. Pound to a purée (use blender).

# My Famous Pies

Two thousand eight hundred and nine pounds worth of bills I owed, back in 1901, when the hotel nearly went bust, and all run up by my husband — former husband — and his cow of a sister, in six short months.

Her buying all her fine clothes and lording it about the place. I must have been out of my mind to think she could have run the housekeeping side of the business. Never lifted a finger in her life, she hadn't, and never had no intentions of doing so from what I could make out. And she had Gus under her thumb.

You wouldn't have thought it humanly possible for anybody to run up such bills, but Gus was never happy and so he took to the bottle. Partly because he knew he'd never have me in the way he wanted to, and partly it was my fault. Buying the Bentinck for him to run was my way of restoring his self-respect, instead it went to his head, and whilst I was busy running the private party-catering side of the business, he was entertaining his friends at the expense of the Bentinck's fine cellar.

'Filling up those pies.'

'Wore mi'self out, I did.'

There was some ripe old language flyin' round the place the night I threw him and his sister Norah out into Duke Street, and a few plants and vases into the bargain. Then I had to sort out the mess; and what a mess! The bedroom trade had dwindled to nothing; any profit I made on cooking up dinners was eaten away — if you'll pardon the phrase — by the losses bein' run up by him and his crowd with their late night parties. All put down to the house account it was, by that Norah.

Well, having made my decision to get rid of him an' her, I then had to sort out how best to pay off them I owed money to, and there were plenty clamouring for payment. The very morning after the shindig I went straight across Duke Street into Jermyn Street and into Mather and Rudd's shop. I'd watched old Mather running his business and I'd noticed he was having problems getting enough quality stuff in the fresh-made side of his business: potted meats, jellied tongues, veal and ham pies, aspic delicacies and such like.

I struck a bargain with him. I'd supply as many veal-and-ham and chicken-and-ham pies as he could sell if he'd knock off the money for doing them from my bill what I owed him.

No sooner said than done. He wasn't no fool. He knew he could sell anything that came out of Louisa Trotter's kitchens to his class of clientèle, all from Mayfair and Belgravia they was. Off I went with me barrow to Smithfield. The best veal, chickens and hams money could buy, I fetched back every morning. Pushed that barrow over every cobble and hole in London, both ways, every day like I said. Up at four o'clock every morning. It was a right sweat, I can tell you. Just me and Mary (Phillips) — she was the only one I'd kept on in the kitchens — stones of flour went into making mountains of hot water crust and every pie was hand-raised round pie moulds. Hundreds and hundreds of them. In and out of the ovens as fast as you liked, and we humped them across Duke Street with our own hands into Old Mather's shop, every day, on the dot, as many as he could sell. I paid me debts off all right, but at the expense of me health. Ended up in the Women's Hospital at Charing Cross. Damn'd nearly didn't come out. If it hadn't been for Charlie Haslemere I don't suppose I'd have found the will or the wherewithal to get the old Bentinck back on its feet. But it's all history now and you all know the story.

# Chicken, Veal and Ham Raised Pie

## Ingredients

*Hot water pastry* (to line a mould or tin 8 inches in diameter, 4 inches deep)
1¼ lbs. plain flour
8 ozs. lard
⅓ pint water

½ teaspoon salt
¼ teaspoon icing sugar
¼ teaspoon ground mace
1 egg-yolk
A little cream or top of the milk

*Filling* 4 full gammon rashers cut ⅛ inch thick
1 3 lb. roasting chicken
1 lb. leg veal
1 teaspoon rubbed sage or 1 tablespoon chopped chives

1 sherry glass Madeira or brandy
1 oz. butter
Salt and freshly ground black pepper
A little lemon juice

Gelatine (see Method)

## Method

*Filling* Skin and strip all the meat off the chicken, leaving the breasts whole. Put the skin and bones into a pan, cover with cold water and simmer for 30 minutes (this stock can be used instead of the jelly).

Mince together the meat from the chicken legs with one of the rashers of ham and half a pound of the veal. Season this with a little sage, salt and pepper, and add the brandy. Work this into a forcemeat.

With a thin-bladed, very sharp knife, cut the chicken breasts into long diagonal slices and cut the veal in a similar way. (You will find this easy to do if you cut on a diagonal plane.)

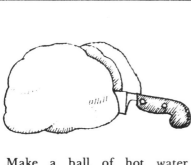

Make a ball of hot water pastry. Cut off 1/3 for the lid and decorations.

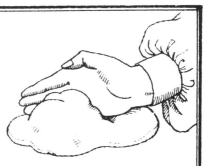

Bang out a round of even thickness with edge of hand keeping fingers together. Leave raised piece in the centre.

Press wooden mould firmly down on raised piece.

Bring pastry up round sides turning and working with floured hands, keeping fingers and thumb closed.

Remove block, trim edge, fill with meat, fit lid, and pinch edges together.

Cut hole in centre, push in a funnel of paper to prevent it closing while cooking. Decorate with pastry leaves.

How to make a hand-raised pie.

*Pastry* Sieve all the dry ingredients together and put into a large bowl making a well in the centre. Melt the lard in the water and bring to the boil. Pour all the liquid, at one fell swoop, into the well made in the flour, then quickly and deftly work this into a soft dough.

Do not over-knead this dough or it will become like elastic and your pastry will be tough, though be it easier to manage! The dough should be warm and soft enough to work with. Reserve ⅓ of the paste for the pie lid. Use the ⅔ to raise a pie shell as illustrated on page 103.

## Pork Pie

### Ingredients

Depending on the size of your pie shell, you will need upwards of the following:

2 lbs. lean leg of pork  
½ lb. pork fat  
   or 2½ lbs. shoulder of  
   pork  
½ lb. green (unsmoked)  
   bacon  

Teaspoon chopped or dried  
   sage  
Salt and pepper (ordinary  
   English white pepper is  
   good for this)  
Squeeze lemon juice  

### Method

Mince the pork, bacon and fat on the *coarse* blade of a mincer. This will ensure a good texture for the pie. Season carefully with salt and pepper, sage and a goodly squeeze of lemon juice for piquancy.

*To make up the pie* Raise the crust as instructed in drawing. Fill the crust to the top. Fit the lid, sealing with beaten egg. Decorate attractively with pastry leaves and flowers. Brush all over with more beaten egg; stand the pie on a baking tray and put in the oven at Gas 6 Elec. 400° for ¾ hour reducing the heat to Gas 3 Elec. 325° for a further hour. Allow the pie to cool before filling with the savoury jelly.

# Jelly for Pork Pie

## Ingredients

2 pig's trotters, chopped
   into pieces
1 knuckle of veal,
   roughly crushed
2 carrots, peeled
   and sliced

2 small onions, peeled
Clove garlic, crushed
4 cloves
Sprig thyme
Dozen peppercorns
5 pints water

## Method

Wash the trotters and bone. Put everything into a large pan, cover with cold water, bring to the boil, despumate, and simmer for 4 hours. Do not add any salt until you have reduced the liquid to approximately one pint.

Allow to cool before pouring into your baked pie.

If you are anxious about the setting quality of the jelly, allow to cool completely, then depending on the strength of the finished jelly, melt it, adding more water or reducing further, whichever is necessary.

# Meat, Game & Poultry

## Tournedos

The tournedos comes from the fillet of beef. A fillet steak is bigger and a bit thicker than a tournedos; a Châteaubriand is three times as big and usually flattened somewhat and served sautéd whole, being *carved* at the table into thin rosey-red strips and served with a Madeira or Béarnaise sauce.

The tournedos was made very popular by the French chefs working in London. At the Bentinck we served ours about 1½ inches thick, tied round their middles with string, to help retain a good shape. We always pan-fried them in butter, but they are excellent char- or even gas-grilled.

Season them *after* cooking, as salting them too early draws the blood. Make sure your pan is searing hot. You will only need enough butter or good olive-oil to prevent the meat sticking.

Seal both sides quickly, then cook to the degree required; *à bleu* (blue or rare), *saignant* (bloody but not rare), or *rosé* (pink or medium).

There'll always be some bandits who'll want it well done — ruined! But that's life.

Here are three of the favourite ways used at the hotel:

# Tournedos Edward VII

Put a tournedos onto a croûton as above, masque with Béarnaise sauce, and top with an artichoke bottom cooked in butter and filled with tiny carrot balls cooked also in butter and sprinkled with freshly chopped tarragon.

# Tournedos Louisa

Grill the tournedos. Brush with French mustard. Coat with a fine creamy onion sauce; top with fresh white breadcrumbs cooked in butter, and mixed with browned flaked almonds.

# Tournedos Alexandra

Make tartlets large enough to contain each tournedos. Fill the tartlets with a purée of mushrooms. Top each tournedos with a half tomato filled with a purée of peas. Serve tomato sauce separately.

# Roast Ribs of Beef with Yorkshire Pudding

Charlie Haslemere's Yorkshire cook learned me how to roast beef like she does and you can't beat it. All my cooks is told to do it this way and the menfolk will give their right arms to get at it when it's rare and ready.

You'll notice a few variations on the pudding recipe, but they come straight from her and good they are too; make a change and keep the customers happy at the same time.

# Preparation for roasting

Score the fat across both ways diagonally, then make a paste with a tablespoon of (unclarified) beef dripping, some salt, ground black pepper, a crushed clove of garlic and a heaped teaspoon of mustard powder. Rub this well into the fat.

Clean, and cut up into small bits, a couple of carrots and a big onion. Put these in the bottom of the roasting tin and stand the ribs — fat side up — on these. They will help towards a good gravy.

Use a good marrow stock to make the gravy which should be

thin, not thickened with flour. A little touch of browning to get a good strong colour is a hint worthwhile accepting as used by all of us in the business, when for one reason or another the natural colour from the brown vegetables isn't good enough; all part of a cook's artists' palate I say, and, whilst we're about it, remember that Roast Beef should always be let stand for 20 minutes or so when it is taken from the oven, before carving, this way it won't shrink as you cut it.

# Yorkshire Pudding

Everybody knows that real Yorkshire Pudding used to be cooked under the meat — the meat was spit-roast wasn't it? Well there's nothing to stop you roasting your meat on a rack and still making the pudding in a tin underneath (you'll have to make the gravy separately though). We can always serve a good pudding at the Bentinck because we don't have no restaurant, just private suites of rooms, so they get it straight from the oven like at home; the only way to my mind. It never did no good — like many cooks and chefs seem to think — to leave it lying around for hours in soggy thick squares, it's got to be all puffed up like a soufflé.

AND, they've got to be made BIG. 7 inch round tins we have at the hotel; one for each plate and served first, before the meat, like what they do up there; their middles filled with good gravy. AND you've got to use some of the drippings from the roasting meat unless you have a good stock of beef drippings in the larder. This should be smoking hot before you pour in the batter.

# Batter

## Ingredients

2 eggs
4 tablespoons flour

¼ pint milk and cold
water mixed

Salt and pepper

## Method 1

Make a well in the flour — break in the eggs. Gradually incor-porate them into the flour before slowly adding the milk and water. Season lightly and beat well. Leave to stand before baking. The batter should be about as thick as coffee cream.

## Method 2

Separate the eggs. Beat the yolks a little, and gradually add the flour thinning down with the milk and water as you go along. Stiffly beat the whites and *mix well in*.

(Extra yolks will make the batter softer; extra white will crisp it up.)

# Variations on Yorkshire Pudding

i When serving with a beef stew, add fried onions to the pudding tin before pouring in the batter.

ii When serving with lamb, add currants or sultanas and freshly chopped mint leaves to the batter.

iii When serving with beef, add freshly grated horseradish or a pinch or two of curry powder to the batter.

iv When serving with roast pork, instead of making a stuffing, add plenty of fried onions to the batter and a good pinch or two of sage and thyme.

# Beef Olives (Olives de Boeuf)

## Ingredients

*For the forcemeat* 8 thin slices top side of beef
4 ozs. finely minced lean veal
2 ozs. minced raw ham
1 teaspoon grated lemon rind

*For the sauce* Oil for frying
1 medium sized onion, finely chopped
1 carrot, peeled and chopped
4 ozs. white mushrooms, quartered
½ teaspoon rubbed thyme

2 ozs butter
1 egg
1 large tablespoon thick cream
Salt and milled pepper
2 heaped tablespoons freshly chopped parsley

1 heaped tablespoon of tomato purée
2 crushed cloves of garlic
1 oz. butter
1 oz. flour
Half a bottle of red wine
¼ pint strong stock
1 large glass port
Freshly chopped green herbs for garnish

Salt and pepper

## Method

Carefully flatten the slices of meat without tearing the flesh. Make up the forcemeat, pounding all the ingredients well in a mortar (or use a blender). Pile the mixture onto the slices of beef and fold into parcels (olives), tie with string across and round to help keep their shape.

Heat the oil in a heavy-bottomed frying pan, fry the vegetables until golden brown, remove with a draining spoon to an ovenproof pot. In the same pan fry the beef olives on all sides until lightly browned. Transfer to pot. Add the butter to the pan, stir in the flour and let this take on a little colour without burning. Add the mushrooms, garlic and thyme, stir well in. Add the tomato purée then the red wine and stock, bring the sauce to the boil and pour over the beef olives. Cover with a lid and cook in a moderate oven for 1-1½ hours.

Take out the beef olives when cooked, with a draining spoon, and arrange on a heated serving dish. Strain the sauce into a clean pan, skim off any excess fat, add the port and strain the sauce again over the waiting beef olives. Sprinkle liberally with freshly chopped herbs and some concasséed tomatoes just before serving.

# The Bentinck Mixed Grill

At the hotel our mixed grills was a speciality, particularly for breakfast; we didn't skimp nothing and each grill was served with a good piece of Bentinck Savoury Butter. This grill sorts out the men from the boys, I can tell you!

## For each guest allow

1 small lamb chop, well
   trimmed and lightly
   seasoned with rosemary
1 small veal chop, well
   trimmed and dredged
   with sage
Small piece of fillet
   steak, well seasoned
   with black pepper
   and garlic

2 chipolata sausages,
   rolled in ground almonds
Rasher of streaky bacon
Calves' kidney, split
   and skewered
Small pieces of calves'
   liver
A whole tomato
Plenty of crisp
   watercress

## Method

Brush your grill pan with good oil, and grill the meats to the degree of rareness requested by the individual guest. Fry the sausages gently in a separate pan, as the almonds burn readily. Do the tomatoes in the same pan. Serve the savoury butter atop some crushed ice in a separate boat.

# Savoury Butter

## Ingredients

| | |
|---|---|
| 4 ozs. good butter | Teaspoon paprika |
| $\frac{1}{4}$ teaspoon ground black pepper | 1 clove garlic, well pounded to a paste |
| $\frac{1}{4}$ teaspoon mild curry powder | A little salt |
| | Teaspoon tomato paste |

## Method

Pound all the ingredients together; form into a sausage, roll in wax paper (or foil) and chill. Cut into discs and serve atop grilled steak or separately.

# Steak, Kidney and Mushroom Pudding

## Ingredients

| | |
|---|---|
| 1$\frac{1}{2}$ lbs. beefsteak | Medium onion |

¾ lb. ox kidney
½ lb. small mushrooms,
   quartered
Salt, pepper and seasoned
   flour
1 bay leaf
Clove garlic, crushed
Suet crust to line and
   lid a 7-inch pudding
   basin (p. 116)
Oil for frying

## Method

Cut the meat into ½ inch cubes. Trim the kidney and cut into similar sized pieces. Roughly chop the onion. Make up the suet crust. Butter the basin and line it with ⅔ of the suet crust reserving the remainder for the lid (the pastry should be about ½ inch thick). Toss the meats in seasoned flour, shaking well of any surplus. Heat a little oil in a frying pan and colour the meat quickly. Now fry the onion until golden brown. Season lightly with salt and pepper and transfer all this to the lined basin. Insert the bay leaf in the centre and sprinkle over the garlic. Pour over enough cold water to just cover the contents. Damp the edges of the suet crust and fit the lid, nipping the edges well together. Cover with a buttered and floured cloth (use foil), tie securely with string, allowing a seam for the crust to rise somewhat during the steaming process.

Set the basin in a large pan of steadily boiling water, cover with a tight fitting lid and steam for 3½ to 4 hours.

Extra gravy can be made from shin beef stewed with a little onion and a few mushroom stalks for 2 to 3 hours.

# Partridges in Cream

Cook without browning in butter one onion chopped and sliced, one carrot, two or three leaves of celery to add flavour, and one bay leaf.

Place in a large stewpan with the partridges, pour over a liqueur glass of brandy and three of chablis, flame it to ensure the right flavour, and add some very strong chicken or game stock to half cover the partridges. Cook for about 40 minutes, then cut partridges neatly in half and place on a dish.

Reduce the stock and add a little cream and milk to make a sauce which is not too thick, pour over the partridges and top with white button mushrooms sliced and cooked in cream. At the last minute garnish with tiny rolls of grilled streaky bacon, and serve with French beans, petits pois, mashed potatoes and purée of celeriac (a root vegetable rather like a potato, which is very tasty served with cream sauce).

# Salmis of Pheasant

## Ingredients

1 pheasant
½ pint brown sauce
  (see p. 84)
6 or 8 slices of
  goose liver
6 or 8 slices of truffle
2 or 3 ozs. butter

2 finely-chopped shallots
¼ teaspoonful of finely
  chopped lemon-rind
¼ teaspoonful of thyme
1 bay leaf
2 glasses of Madeira
  or Marsala wine
Salt and pepper

## Method

Pluck, draw and truss the bird for roasting. Baste it well with hot butter, roast in a quick oven for 30 minutes, basting frequently, then strain the butter used for basting into a stewpan.

Divide the bird into neat joints, put the breast, wings and legs aside, and cut the remainder into small pieces. Re-heat the butter in the stewpan, put in the small pieces of pheasant, add the lemon-rind, shallots, bay leaf and thyme, fry well, then drain off the butter, return the pieces of pheasant to the stewpan. Heat up the brown sauce in a stewpan, add to it the wine, season to taste, and simmer for 10 minutes, then put in the pheasant. Meanwhile, re-heat the butter, fry the slices of liver, and drain them well.

Arrange the pheasant in a silver or earthenware casserole, or stewpan, interspersed with slices of liver and truffle; pour the sauce over, garnish with glazed croûtons of fried bread, and serve hot.

# Louisa Trotter's Quail Pudding

## Ingredients

*The filling* 8 quail
8 thin slices of topside
  of beef
4 rashers of streaky
  bacon

4 ozs. mushrooms
2 onions
Salt and pepper
Stock to cover, or half stock
  and half red wine

## Method

*The crust Method 1*
8 ozs. self-raising flour
1 level teaspoon baking powder
4 ozs. suet
Salt
Freshly ground white
  pepper
Pinch of powdered mace
Powdered rosemary or
  powdered bay leaf
Cold water to mix

*Method 2*
8 ozs. self-raising flour
3 ozs. suet
2 ozs. grated cold hard
  butter
1 teaspoon grated lemon rind
Salt
Freshly ground white
  pepper
Lemon juice and water
  to mix

## Method

Grease a 3 pint basin with butter, sprinkle with grated

nutmeg. Sieve the flour, salt and pepper and spices. Lightly toss in the suet (and lemon rind and grated butter if you are using Method 2). Stir loosely with a fork or 'rain' the dry ingredients through the fingers until thoroughly mixed. Make a well in the centre, and add the liquid in one fell swoop. Gather the ingredients together, kneading as little as possible, until the dough is a workable mass.

Have your steamer or pan ready with boiling water. Dredge a baking board and rolling pin with flour, and roll out two-thirds of the crust as thinly as possible. Line the basin, letting the crust hang over the edge.

Cut the bacon rashers in half lengthways and wrap strips round each quail. Cut the beef into strips and season lightly. Chop the onions and mushrooms. Place all the ingredients in the lined basin. Cover with the stock, or half stock and half red wine.

Roll out the remaining crust into a round, wet the edges of the lining pastry, and fit the top on. Cover loosely with a pudding cloth or foil, and steam for 2½ hours either in a steamer or in a pan with a tight-fitting lid. If you use the pan method, keep the water at least two-thirds to three-quarters up the sides of the basin, and keep it boiling gently — just one stage further on than simmering. If you use a steamer, the water should boil at a steady rate and will need constant topping up.

# Pigeon Pie

## Ingredients

3 plump pigeons
6 rashers streaky bacon
12 ozs. minced pork
    (fat and lean)
Small onion
Knob of butter for
    frying

$\frac{1}{4}$ teaspoon ground thyme
$\frac{1}{4}$ teaspoon ground sage
Salt and black pepper
Stock (see Method)
$\frac{1}{2}$ pint red wine
Short crust or suet pastry
    to cover pie dish

## Method

Remove the breasts from the pigeons; skin these. Remove
whatever meat you can from the legs, put this together with
the bones into a pan, cover with cold water, add a bouquet of
herbs, simmer for an hour to make a good strong stock. Strain
this and reduce in quantity until you have approx. $\frac{3}{4}$ pint.
Take the six breasts, and flatten them somewhat. Mince
together the pork and the onion, seasoning lightly with the
herbs, salt and pepper. Spread this mixture onto the flattened
breasts and roll them up, securing with a small stick. Wrap
each breast in a rasher of bacon; melt the butter in a frying
pan and gently brown the wrapped breasts on all sides. Place
the browned breasts in a shallow lidded pan in one layer, pour
over the red wine and as much stock as is necessary to just
cover them. Season lightly. Braise the breasts until they are
just tender — about an hour will do. Leave them to cool
before transferring them to a pie dish — again in one layer —
pour over some of the gravy and cover with a good crust. Bake
in a hot oven until the crust is cooked and golden brown. Any
extra gravy can be served separately.

(If a lightly thickened gravy is preferred — a little butter
mixed with flour can be whisked into the liquid whilst they are
braising.)

# Côtelettes de Bécassines
## à la Souvaroff

This is a snipe dish, named after a Russian prince.

Take 8 snipe, bone except for the leg bones, and put the 2 cutlets each makes, on a dish. Season with pepper and salt, pour a drop of brandy on the top of each, spread with a little farce (forcemeat) of game about half-an-inch thick, then a slice of foie gras a quarter-of-an-inch thick, then more forcemeat. Gently place each cutlet in a pig's caul, wrap and brush over with yolk of egg and breadcrumbs. Grill both sides until brown.

Serve on a silver dish bordered with potatoes and forcemeat, heaping in the centre beans, truffles and mushrooms. Serve with madeira sauce made with small slices of truffle.

# Jugged Hare

Now don't go thinking you can make a proper jugged hare without using the blood; it just won't be right. Here's how I jug my hares, using a good brown English hare, though I've made a good dish or two using blue hares from Scotland, so take your pick.

# Ingredients

1 hare cut up into pieces
2 tablespoons oil or
  bacon fat
2 onions stuck with 2 or
  3 cloves
½ teaspoon ground black
  pepper
¼ small head celery,
  sliced
1 teaspoon allspice
1 large carrot, peeled
  and sliced

Juice of 2 Seville oranges
2 inch piece of orange
  rind
1½ pints brown stock
¼ pint Ruby or Tawny port
1 tablespoon redcurrant
  jelly
Bouquet garni
Salt
Butter and flour paste
  *(beurre manié)*
Fried forcemeat balls

Blood of the hare

# Method

Marinate the pieces of hare (p.121). Pat dry and fry until brown on all sides in the oil. Pack into an ovenpot, and add the vegetables, herbs, spices, bouquet. Barely cover with stock. Seal the lid with flour and water paste. Cook in a slow oven (Gas 3 Elec. 325°) for 3 hours.

Strain the gravy into a saucepan. Whisk in enough butter and flour paste *(beurre manié)* to make a sauce the consistency of thin cream. Add the port and jelly. Take a ladleful of the hot sauce and stir this into the blood; now pour this back into the sauce. Check seasoning. Re-heat, strain over the waiting pieces of hare, and garnish with fried forcemeat balls.

*Note* For those who don't wish to use a blood liaison, add a little extra butter paste, but the sauce will not be so rich and dark.

# Marinade for game

## Ingredients

$\frac{1}{4}$ pint red wine
  (or strong beer)
2 tablespoons olive oil
2 fresh bay leaves
2 shallots or small
  onion

1 doz. crushed juniper
  berries
Salt and freshly milled
  black pepper
$\frac{1}{4}$ teaspoon each of thyme,
  sage, marjoram

## Method

Bring all the ingredients to the boil, simmer for 3 minutes. Cool *completely* before pouring over the meats to be marinated.

Turn the meat pieces frequently whilst they are 'soaking'. Allow 12 to 24 hours for this to be effective.

The marinade can be reduced by half (by rapid boiling) and used where appropriate.

# Quail with Grapes

## Ingredients

10 quail
4 ozs. butter, melted
1 lb. skinned and pipped
  green grapes

$\frac{1}{2}$ pint brown sauce (p. 84)
$\frac{1}{4}$ pint dry white wine
Juice of half a lemon
Salt and pepper

## Method

Arrange the quail in a braising pan just large enough to contain them; season lightly, pour over the melted butter,

121

cover with a lid and braise in a very hot oven for 20 minutes (remove the lid for the last 5 minutes to let the quail colour nicely).

Arrange the quail on a serving dish. Scatter with the grapes and put to keep hot. Place the pan on the stove; allow the juices to 'settle', pour away excess fat. Add the white wine and reduce this by half. Add the brown sauce, simmer gently for 5 minutes. Season with lemon juice, pour over the waiting quail and serve.

# Roast Stuffed Shoulder of Lamb

## Ingredients

| | |
|---|---|
| A shoulder of lamb | 1 oz. butter |
| Veal forcemeat | $\frac{3}{4}$ oz. flour |
| (see p.126) | 2 or 3 ozs. dripping |
| $\frac{3}{4}$ pint stock | Salt and pepper |

## Method

Remove the bones and boil them for at least 1 hour for stock. Flatten the meat with a cutlet-bat or heavy knife, season well with salt and pepper, and spread on the forcemeat. Roll up lightly, tie securely with string, and place in a baking-tin in which the dripping has been previously melted.

Baste well, put it into a moderate oven, and cook gently for about $1\frac{1}{4}$ hours, basting frequently. Meanwhile fry the butter and flour together until well browned, add the prepared stock, stir until boiling, and season to taste. Remove the meat and keep it hot, pour off the fat without disturbing the sediment in the tin, and add the brown sauce. Replace the meat, and cook it gently for 20 minutes longer, basting frequently meanwhile. Serve with a little sauce poured over the meat, and send the remainder to table in a tureen.

# Sweetbreads à ma façon

Veal sweetbreads may be counted as one of the greatest delicacies from the butcher's shop. They appear as an entrée and can be braised, poached, grilled, creamed or crumbed and fried.

## Ingredients

3 pairs calves' sweetbreads
Flour to dredge
4 ozs. butter
Glass of medium dry sherry
2 teaspoons tomato purée
2 teaspoons potato flour
  *(fécule)*

½ pint chicken stock
Salt and pepper
¼ teaspoon rosemary
Clove garlic, crushed
2 lbs. fresh spinach
¼ pint sour cream
2 ozs. butter

Salt and pepper

## Method

Cover sweetbreads with water, bring to the boil, drain and rinse under cold running water for 10 minutes. Drain again. Dry the breads well between the folds of a clean towel pressed with a board.

Trim the breads of all membranes. Slice them into two or three diagonal slices. Dredge lightly with flour. Season lightly with salt and pepper. Heat the butter in a shallow pan until foaming. Brown the sliced breads quickly. Pour over the sherry and let it catch alight.

Lift the breads from the pan; work into the juices the purée and potato flour. Add the stock, stir until the sauce boils. Add the rosemary and garlic. Return the breads to the pan and simmer them in the sauce for 20 minutes.

Wash and pick the spinach. Melt 2 ozs. of butter in a large pan. Add the spinach; season lightly with salt and pepper. Fit a lid and toss frequently until the juices 'draw'. Cook the spinach in its own juices for 7 to 10 minutes. Drain well, pressing out any surplus liquid. Chop very finely. Stir in the sour cream. Mound the purée into a warm dish; arrange the sweetbreads along the top and pour over the hot sauce.

# Braised Duck with Chestnuts

## Ingredients

1 duck
1 pint stock
¾ pint Espagnole sauce
    (see p.84)
1 glass of port wine
    (optional)

1 dessertspoonful of
    redcurrant jelly
1 Spanish onion
1 lb. of chestnuts
Larding bacon
1 egg

*For the mirepoix, or
    foundation:* 2 ozs. of
    butter
2 onions
2 carrots
1 small turnip

2 cloves
2 strips of celery
A bouquet garni (parsley,
    thyme, bay leaf)
Teaspoon allspice
Salt and pepper

## Method

Boil the chestnuts and remove the skins, cook the Spanish onion in stock or water until tender, chop both finely, season with salt and pepper, add the egg, and use these for stuffing the duck. Truss the duck and lard it neatly. Put the butter and sliced vegetables into a large stewpan, place the duck on the top of them, cover and fry gently for 20 minutes. Next add as much of the stock as will three-quarter cover the vegetables, and the remainder as that in the stewpan boils away. Cover the duck with a buttered paper, put on the lid, and cook gently for about 2 hours, or until the duck is perfectly tender.

Heat the Espagnole sauce, add to it the wine (if used) and

jelly, and season to taste. Remove the trussing strings, and put the duck in a hot oven for a few minutes to crisp the bacon. Serve with a small quantity of the sauce poured over, and the remainder in a sauce-boat.

# An Old English 'Ragoo' of Kidneys

## Ingredients

6 calves' kidneys (ox, lambs', or pigs' will do, but don't have the same delicate flavour)
4 ozs. mushrooms
Small onion, finely chopped
Clove garlic, crushed

2 ozs. butter
Scant teaspoon flour
$\frac{1}{4}$ pint cream
$\frac{1}{4}$ teaspoon powdered ginger
Small glass dry sherry
Salt and freshly milled
  pepper

## Method

Skin and trim kidneys, *slice* them as thinly as possible. Clean and slice mushrooms. Peel and *slice* the onion. (All this slicing gives an interesting texture to the finished dish.)

Melt butter in a shallow pan or frying pan; add onion, and allow to acquire a golden colour. Remove with a draining spoon to a plate.

Now fry off the kidneys a few pieces at a time, adding more butter if necessary. Remove these whilst you fry off the mushrooms quickly. Sprinkle over the modicum of flour and ginger; stir well in. Add the sherry and cream; bring to the boil and cook for a minute or so until smooth.

Return the kidneys and onions to the pan to heat through. Don't let them boil or they will toughen.

Serve as instructed above.

# Veal Forcemeat

## Ingredients

½ lb. lean veal
¼ lb. finely chopped
   beef suet
2 ozs. fat bacon cut
   into fine strips
2 tablespoonsful of
   freshly made breadcrumbs

1 dessertspoonful of
   finely chopped parsley
½ teaspoonful
   finely chopped onion
2 eggs
Salt and pepper
Pinch of ground mace

Pinch of nutmeg

## Method

Pass the veal twice through the mincing machine, then pound it and the suet and bacon well in the mortar. Pass through a wire sieve, add the rest of the ingredients, season to taste, and use.

# Ragoût of Lamb with Spinach

## Ingredients

2 or 3 lb. of neck or
   breast of lamb
½ pint of boiling stock
2 ozs. butter
1 oz. flour
1 onion
1 small carrot
1 strip celery

A bouquet garni (parsley,
   thyme, bay leaf)
1 egg-yolk
1 tablespoonful of cream
¼ pint spinach purée
   mixed with the juice
   of half a lemon
Salt and pepper

# Method

Trim the meat, and blanch it by putting it into cold water, bring slowly to the boil, then immerse it for a few minutes in seasoned salt water. Drain, dry well, and cut into 2 inch squares.

Heat the butter in a stewpan, and fry the sliced vegetables for 15 minutes, but do not let them brown. Now sprinkle in the flour, stir and cook for 3 or 4 minutes, then add the boiling stock, herbs, $\frac{1}{4}$ teaspoonful of salt, $\frac{1}{2}$ the quantity of pepper, and stir until smooth. Lay the pieces of meat in the sauce, put on the lid, which should fit closely, and simmer very gently for about $1\frac{1}{2}$ hours.

Meanwhile cook the spinach, rub it through a fine sieve, and season to taste. When the meat is ready, pile it in the centre of a hot dish. Strain the sauce into another stewpan, and add the spinach purée. When nearly boiling put in the yolk of egg and cream, previously mixed together, and stir until the sauce thickens.

Season to taste, pour over the meat, and serve.

# Lamb Stew

The French call this a *navarin,* but this is the Bentinck version which we always find popular with the menfolk at lunchtime.

## Ingredients

| | |
|---|---|
| 2 lbs. middle neck of lamb | 1 tablespoon seasoned flour (see method) |
| 2 large onions | $\frac{1}{2}$ pint water |
| 2 large carrots | $\frac{1}{2}$ pint dry white wine |
| 1 small turnip | Bouquet of herbs |
| 2 tablespoons oil for frying | 1 clove of garlic, crushed |
| | A little sugar |

Plenty of freshly chopped parsley and chives

## Method

Trim the pieces of meat, cut the onions into largish pieces. Cut the carrots and turnips into even-sized $\frac{1}{2}$ inch shaped sticks. Heat the oil, dredge the meat with seasoned flour and fry it until lightly browned on all sides. Remove the meat to an ovenproof pot and fry the vegetables in the same pan, adding more oil if necessary, until they too are golden brown. During this process add a sprinkling of sugar and dredge over the remaining flour. Pour in the water and wine, bring to the boil then pour over the waiting pieces of meat. Season lightly, add the bouquet and garlic, cook in a moderate oven for an hour or until the meat is tender. Sprinkle the dish with parsley and chives just before serving.

# Tripe and Onions

## Ingredients

2 lbs. dressed tripe cut
   into 2 inch squares
2 large onions, sliced
4 ozs. butter
$\frac{1}{2}$ pint milk

$\frac{1}{2}$ pint water
$\frac{1}{4}$ pint thin cream
1 tablespoon flour
Salt, pepper (or nutmeg)
Freshly chopped parsley

## Method

Bring the pieces of tripe to the boil in water, drain well.

Soften the onions in the butter, add the tripe pieces, and the milk and water. Salt lightly. Simmer in a low oven for 2 hours.

Mix the flour and cream together, pour into the cooked tripe stirring well. Simmer for a further 20 minutes. Season carefully with pepper or nutmeg. Pour into a serving dish. Sprinkle with parsley and serve.

# Rabbit Sauté

## Ingredients

1 rabbit
3 ozs. bacon fat
  (or butter or oil)
3 onions }
3 carrots } chopped
2 ozs. flour

½ pint stock
½ pint white wine
2 ozs. tomato purée
Clove of garlic, crushed
Bouquet garni
Salt and pepper

Chopped parsley and chives

## Method

Joint the rabbit into 2 shoulders, the legs into 2 pieces, the trunk into 5 or 6 pieces. Brown the pieces on all sides in smoking fat. Remove to an oven pot. Fry the vegetables in the same fat until light brown; sprinkle with flour, add the wine, stock and purée and garlic and bouquet garni. Season lightly. Pour over rabbit pieces; cook in oven until tender. Sprinkle with the fresh herbs just before serving.

# Chicken Rissoles

## Ingredients

4 ozs. cooked chicken
2 ozs. cooked ham or
  tongue
4 button mushrooms
1 small truffle
½ oz. butter
½ oz. flour

¼ pint white stock
1 tablespoonful of
  cream or milk
Salt and pepper to taste
Egg
Breadcrumbs
Frying fat

Rough puff-paste

# Method

Chop the chicken and ham finely, cut the mushrooms and truffle into small dice. Melt the butter in a stewpan, stir in the flour, add the stock, stir and boil well.

Put in the chicken and ham, season to taste, mix the ingredients well over the fire, then add the mushrooms, truffle, and cream or milk, and put aside to cool. Roll out the paste as thinly as possible — stamp it out into rounds of about 2 inches in diameter, pile a teaspoonful of the preparation in the centre, wet the edges with water, place another round of paste on the top, and press the edges together neatly, Brush over with egg and cover with breadcrumbs, and fry until lightly browned in hot fat.

If preferred, half the quantity of the meat mixture may be enclosed in one round of paste, one half of which must be folded over to form them into half-moon shapes; variety may be introduced by substituting crushed vermicelli for the breadcrumbs.

# Chicken Ramekins

## Ingredients

6 ozs. raw chicken
2 tablespoonsful of cream
2 yolks of eggs
2 whites of eggs

$\frac{1}{2}$ oz. butter
2 mushrooms
1 truffle
Salt and pepper

Sauce, if liked

## Method

Shred the chicken meat finely, or pass it through a mincing machine, then pound it well in the mortar, adding by degrees the yolks of 2 eggs. Season well, and rub through a fine wire sieve. Whip the cream slightly, and whisk the whites of eggs to a stiff froth, and then add with the mushrooms and truffle cut into small dice, to the chicken purée. Mix lightly together, if too stiff add a little milk, and put the mixture into 8 well-buttered china or paper ramekin cases. The cases should not be more than three parts filled, as the mixture rises considerably in baking.

Place the cases on a baking-sheet, and cook them in a moderate oven for about 20 minutes. Serve in the cases, and, if liked, send hot Béchamel or other suitable sauce to table in a sauce-boat.

# Chicken with Parsley

## Ingredients

1 chicken
Parsley

Seasoning
Lemon

## Method

Stuff a chicken with heads of parsley. Fill very full and season well. Roast the chicken, basting it well, and serve with parsley sauce.

This can be poured over the cut-up bird. Garnish with sprigs of fresh parsley and thin lemon rounds.

# Parsley Sauce

## Ingredients

2 large handfuls of
  parsley

$\frac{3}{4}$ pint cream

## Method

Put the parsley in a saucepan, season it, cover it with cream and cook it very slowly by the side of the above for 2 hours. Strain and serve.

# When the King Comes

There's not much what'll make me shiver in me boots I can tell you, not at my age now, what with all I've lived through and seen, the work I've put away at the hotel, me money struggles, not to mention nature's little interferences now and then in the form of those members of the opposite sex what seem to think they was God-blessed and put on earth to muck around with ladies' affections! I'm not complaining on that score, mind you, it's just that it all takes its toll even though it's said it helps build character.

'Louisa my girl,' I used to say to myself, 'there's no use crying all over the place, only makes things untidy and gets you nowhere in the end, and you look a right sight for everybody else to behold!' My philosophy's always been to look forwards; never backwards, *that* never got nobody nowhere. I'm not saying there hasn't been times when I've near panicked, but a few deep breaths (or perhaps a glass of bubbly these days) gets you ready to work out a plan of action. Life has to be planned in the hotel business, and given a bit of a push at times because

'When the King comes . . .'

every day's different. Different people and different problems dealing with them. What they'll eat and what they'll drink, what sort of flowers they like, how many blankets on their beds, even to which way they want the bleedin' bed to face! We get 'em all at the Bentinck, a right mixing of society crosses our portals, but most of them are of me own choosing. We've seen them all except journalists that is. Like I've said before, I can't do with them pokin' their bleedin' noses everywhere, prying into people's business, a real load of snoopers they are and I don't like 'em around, particularly with the delicate situation with regard to Himself (H.M. Edward VII) when he decides to pay us a visit at the hotel. Since him and me got all 'that side' of things sorted out he's become a real pal, and it's a dimwitted hostess what doesn't ask Louisa Trotter to cook up a dinner for her — if she wants the royal presence that is. People are learning that they can climb their way into Society on the shoulders of a good cook, and *that* I am. The old lad seems to have taken a shine to the Bentinck at last and every now an' then I get a call from his equerry telling me what time he wants to dine and how many there'll be. It's never all men, probably eight or ten people, half and half with Mrs Keppel taking pride of place! The choice of menu and the wines left to me. I knew what he liked didn't I? I regret to say that our King Edward was a right bit of a glutton, he'd even have a lobster mayonnaise at tea-time (afternoon tea-time, I mean as well) when everybody else was making do with toasted crumpets, scones, sandwiches and cakes. Then a twelve course dinner wasn't unheard of *and* I've left chafing-dishes of devilled chicken and piles of well-filled sandwiches for them all to dig into after they'd played their rubbers of bridge!

They got a better deal all round at the Bentinck. None of your usual society set-up where pompous old bores woofed and barked at each other and the women prattled on like puffed-up hens in a coop.

Not that He tolerated much of that nonsense. The Queen (Victoria) had kept him out of all State business even though he was prepared to accept his responsibilities. This gave him the time and the energy to get abroad, look around and learn to enjoy himself. And he did. And stylishly. When he was

Prince of Wales, his Marlborough House Set was a far cry from the stuffy German lot that slunk around Buckingham Palace and Windsor Castle. It must have been this lot what helped him keep his thick accent. I used to pull his leg about that rolled 'r' of his. Came right from his lacquered boots. I couldn't half make him laugh about it, being a bit of a mimic myself. I think now, that's what he liked about me more than 'the other' thing; my sense of humour. I suppose we all forget that the 'Edwardian' period and style began in the 1870s, long before he got his little bum on the throne. He liked to dress up, and paid the best tailors in London to help him do this. Had special clothes for everything he did, and everywhere he went, races, yachting, South of France, theatre, opera and the music hall. There hadn't never been a royal like him before, and I can't think there ever will be. The would-be fashionables followed everything he did, and London wasn't the only place under his influence, any European capital he visited took on a bit of his style after he'd paid them a visit. I was a bit ruffled when I heard from César (Ritz) that Himself had made his first public appearance in a London restaurant at the Carlton Hotel. Mind you, I'd had a good crack at the whip with all my private parties where he'd been, and it didn't take him long to realise that at the Bentinck he could dine comfortable and incognito when he wanted. One thing Louisa Trotter and her staff are, and that's masters of discretion. Nobody ever bothers my guests because nobody ever finds out who's in the place. But when we know he's coming, I'll admit we all get a bit extra worked up, not as much as I was that first time I cooked for him.

When I think back I come all over cold — even though I didn't know he was the honoured guest until I'd finished cooking the dinner up. It seems like a world away now. How I coped with it all and the mishaps, like when Ivy — she was a bitchy one that one — they come in all sizes — banged into Mary and made her drop my special tray of grouse. But our poisoned Ivy hadn't bargained on me always being prepared for eventualities. I'd plenty more in the oven, they'd only to have their garnishes fixed and we sent them up before Gus (Augustus Trotter who I married later, and was butler in the house) noticed anything was wrong.

What a dinner that was. Do you know, I sometimes think it was the best dinner I ever cooked up. My consommé was clear as crystal. The turbot was a beauty. Ten pounds it weighed in its shimmy and I can picture that big pot of black Beluga caviar to this day, spoonsful piled on one half of a lemon slice, red salmon caviar on the other half, then all set down the spine of the fish. Dredged hard-boiled egg yolks and whites were sifted over the rest of the fish to look like marble.

Monsieur Alex (Lord Henry Norton's chef de cuisine) had always insisted on sauces being sieved first, then tammied (squeezed through a fine linen cloth), and I even did this with my bread sauce for the grouse. As fine as face cream I like it to be. With a touch of garlic and nutmeg just noticeable, but necessary.

Timing asparagus can be tricky particularly if you're knocking up a hollandaise sauce to go with it, but that night the angels were on my side.

My pears in lemon juice have never come better, the syrup just clinging to the flesh and the thin fronds of peel nicely crystallised. We had a few glasses of bubbly that night to celebrate when it was all cleared up.

'To Miss Leyton and her staff, may I add my congratulations to those of His Royal Highness, The Prince of Wales.' Gus proposed a toast I'll never forget, on a night I'm not likely to forget either am I?

# King Edward's Grouse

Whenever we wanted to dress up a dish specially there was one or two things we could turn to, to make things look really grand.

There has to be a splendid dish to start off with. Doesn't matter whether it's gold, silver or just plain pot; but big and stylish it's got to be!

Then — for the special grouse we used to cook up for H.M. — we lifted these on socles made in this instance from wedges of fried bread.

The grouse were perched on top of these and we'd set either a big centre decoration in the middle of all the grouse: feathers and rowan berries all wired up to look magnificent, with the tips of the feathers brushed with gilt, or we'd stick individual hâtelets (skewers) into each one. These were made of silver and came with unusual fancy tops. Then we'd arrange plenty of fresh watercress round the base, and we had a beautiful presentation for the table.

# Roasting the Grouse

The main problem when roasting most game birds is keeping them moist. You've got to have your birds well hung to break down the tissues so's they don't need too long in the oven.

I'm not all that keen on the glorious 12th bag: mind you, they're usually young — but you can never be too sure of their state 'til it's too late.

This is how I roast my grouse. For each grouse you will need a quarter of a small onion, a bit of bay leaf, two rashers of bacon, and some butter, salt and pepper. Wrap a small rasher of bacon round a piece of onion and put this inside the bird, with a ½ inch of bay leaf. Brush the birds all over with plenty of melted butter, and twine another piece of bacon round the breast. Season each one lightly.

Melt some more butter in the type of pan which can end up in the oven. When it's foaming and gone quiet — which butter does when it gets to the 'nutty flavoured' stage, brown each bird on all sides. Transfer the pan to a very hot oven and roast quickly (45 minutes maximum).

You cannot beat serving them in the traditional way with freshly made game chips or straw potatoes, a creamy, smooth, well-flavoured bread sauce and a good giblet gravy.

*Giblet Gravy* Gently brown the giblets of a brace of grouse

The King's Grouse

in some butter. Sprinkle over them a heaped teaspoon of flour, and let this take on a brown colour. Pour over a good glass of brandy, and flame it. Now pour over a pint of cold water. Simmer for 45 minutes. Strain. Leave on one side until required.

When the grouse are cooked, but still pink and the inside juices still somewhat bloody when the birds are held up with a fork (pierced *underneath)*, dress them on your dish. Remove the onion and bacon from inside each bird, and fry these in the pan juices. Pour another glass of brandy into the roasting pan, and collect all the sediment, onion and juices together. Pour in the made basic gravy. Give it a quick boil, strain into a small pan. Let it 'settle', skim off any excess fat; re-heat, check seasoning, and serve in a silver boat.

# Fish

## Boiled Turbot and Butter Sauce

Whole turbot were usual in Edwardian times, the white skin being considered a delicacy, particularly by the men in the household.

Fillets of turbot can be substituted, or any other firm-fleshed white fish may be used (Halibut, Haddock, etc.)

Allow 6 ozs. of filleted fish per serving, or 8 ozs. on the bone. Select a shallow pan just large enough to contain the fillets when folded, or if the fish is thicker, the whole pieces. Butter the base of the pan, and cut a circle of kitchen paper just large enough to fit the surface of the fish. Butter this.

Make up a court bouillon as follows: to each pint of water add a tablespoon of white wine vinegar, a small piece of onion and carrot, a tablespoon of oil, salt and a dozen peppercorns, half a bay leaf. Bring all these ingredients to the boil, and simmer for 15 minutes. *Allow to cool,* then strain the liquor over the waiting fish pieces. Cover with the buttered paper and a lid; bring to the boil, reduce the heat to an absolute minimum, and poach the fish until just tender. Remove the pieces with a fish slice, drain on a clean towel, pour over a *little* melted butter. Arrange on a white napkin on a serving dish, and garnish.

*For the garnish* Lemon slices, Black caviare (or lumpfish roe), freshly chopped parsley, hard-boiled egg.

If you possess a 'canelle' knife, it is pretty to incise the sides of the lemon so that when it is cut it will look more attractive.

Spoon caviare over half the lemon slices, arrange rows of sieved hard-boiled egg yolk, parsley and sieved egg whites down the spine of the fish.

# Butter Sauce

The quality of this sauce depends entirely on the quality of the butter used.

## Ingredients

| | |
|---|---|
| 4 ozs. unsalted butter | $\frac{1}{4}$ pint milk |
| Level dessertspoon flour | 1 tablespoon lemon juice |

Salt and freshly milled *white* pepper (black leaves specks)

## Method

Cut the butter into smallish cubes and work the flour into this until you have a soft paste. Transfer this to a small pan. Over a minimum heat beat this mixture until it starts to melt, then gradually add the milk, beating all the time. *Simmer* for 2 minutes, and then add a light seasoning, but be fairly bold with the lemon juice.

Unsalted butter has a totally different flavour to salted, but leaves the options open, adjust the seasoning when appropriate.

# Blanchaille

Lord Henry Norton would have had these for breakfast, luncheon and dinner if he'd had a chance. We were always bringing a few pints of whitebait back from Billingsgate. (Whitebait, like cockles and mussels, were sold by the pint at fishmongers, as they were so cheap it was a quick and easy way of measuring them.)

## Method

Ideally they should just be picked over and not washed. Roll them, a few at a time, in seasoned flour and fry in lightly smoking fat in a frying basket for 2 to 3 minutes. Drain them well on crumpled paper.

Finally, re-heat the fat until smoking again and plunge the whole lot in for a minute to crisp them up.

Drain and shake well. Serve dished on a clean napkin. Brown bread and butter and lemon wedges are the usual accompaniment.

# Devilled Whitebait

Proceed as above, but dredge with cayenne pepper after the final frying.

# Salmon Pudding

This is a good Scotch receipt from Eliza Acton and can be served hot or cold. Pound or chop small, or rub through a sieve (blender) one pound of cold boiled salmon freed entirely from bone and skin; and blend it lightly but thoroughly with half-a-pound of fine breadcrumbs, a teaspoonful of essence of anchovies, a quarter of a pint of cream, a seasoning of fine salt and cayenne, and four well whisked eggs. Press the mixture closely and evenly into a deep dish or mould, buttered in every part, and bake it for one hour in a moderate oven.

Salmon, 1 lb; breadcrumbs, $\frac{1}{2}$ lb; essence of anchovies, 1 teaspoonful; cream, $\frac{1}{4}$ pint; eggs, 4; salt and cayenne; baked 1 hour.

This is such an excellent receipt from Eliza Acton's pen, it was used daily at the Bentinck in the salmon season. Bake it in a *bain-marie*. It is much improved when served with a light Mousseline sauce (two-thirds Hollandaise sauce, one-third half-whipped cream).

# Grilled Salmon

I couldn't instruct you how to grill salmon better than Agnes Marshall does.

If you have a charcoal grill then all the better, as you'll get a good 'grilled' flavour.

Of course, with modern grills you won't be needing those straws she talks about, but it shows her cleverness and attention to detail; she wasn't going to have her fish sticking and getting all broke up.

## Method

Take slices of salmon $1\frac{1}{2}$ to 2 inches thick, season them with coralline pepper (paprika), salt, and salad oil. If the salmon is left in the oil for an hour or so before grilling, it would be more moist when cooked; if the slices are cut to the extreme thickness they should be wrapped in paper oiled on both sides, especially if the fire is very fierce. This paper can be dispensed with when the slices are not so thick. Warm the grill and rub it over with oil before using it, then arrange on it a dozen or sixteen oiled straws a little longer than the slices of salmon, place the salmon on these and put to grill over a clear fire, keeping the grill somewhat slanting to prevent the fire smoking. It is best to have the grill rather near the fire, otherwise the fish is likely to be soft and flabby when cooked.

Keep the slices well basted with clarified butter or salad oil. They should only be turned once in the cooking, and the slices, about 1½ inches thick, will take 10 to 15 minutes, according to the fire. When done they should be a pretty golden brown on the top and bottom, perfectly crisp and firm, and without a split in the skin. Carefully remove the paper, if used, and serve on a very hot dish, with or without a dish-paper.

The best way to baste is with a paste brush dipped in oil or butter. Garnish with a little parsley and serve with cold Verte sauce in a sauceboat. If cooked in front of the fire in a double grill, the slices should have a layer of straws on each side of them. Salmon cooked in this way may be served with many sauces, such as Verte, Tartare, etc.

# Mackerel Stewed with Wine

*An Eliza Acton recipe* Work very smoothly together a large teaspoonful of flour with two ounces of butter, put them into a stewpan, and stir or shake them round over the fire until the butter is dissolved; add a quarter of a teaspoonful of mace, twice as much salt, and some cayenne; pour in by slow degrees three glasses of claret; and when the sauce boils, lay in a couple of fine mackerel well cleaned, and wiped quite dry; stew them very softly from fifteen to twenty minutes, and turn them when half done; lift them out, and dish them carefully; stir a teaspoonful of made mustard to the sauce, give it a boil, and pour it over the fish. When more convenient, substitute port wine (or any other red wine) and a little lemon juice for the claret.

Mackerel, 2; flour, 1 teaspoonful; butter, 2 ozs; seasoning of salt, mace, and cayenne; claret, 3 wine-glassfuls; made mustard, 1 teaspoonful; 15-20 minutes.

(This is excellent when cooked with half dry white wine and half white port: I also used a mild French or German mustard. Use a shallow lidded sauté pan.)

# Mackerel Broiled Whole

*An Eliza Acton recipe* Empty and cleanse perfectly a fine and very fresh mackerel, but without opening it more than is needful; dry it well, either in a cloth or by hanging it in cool air until it is stiff. Make with a sharp knife a deep incision the whole length of the fish on either side of the back bone, and about half an inch from it, and with a feather, put in a little cayenne and fine salt, mixed with a few drops of good salad oil or clarified butter. Lay the mackerel over a moderate fire upon a well-beaten grid-iron which has been rubbed with suet; loosen it gently should it stick, which it will do unless often moved; and when it is equally done on both sides, turn the back to the fire. About half an hour will broil it well. If a sheet of thickly-buttered writing-paper be folded round it, and just twisted at the ends before it is laid on the gridiron, it will be finer eating than if exposed to the fire; but sometimes when this is done, the skin will adhere to the paper, and be drawn off with it, which injures its appearance. A cold *Maître d'Hôtel* sauce may be put into the back before it is sent to table. This is one of the very best modes of dressing a mackerel, which in flavour is quite a different fish when thus prepared to one which is simply boiled. A drop of oil is sometimes passed over the skin to prevent its sticking to the iron. It may be laid to the fire after having been merely cut as we have directed, when it is preferred so.

30 minutes; 25 if *small*.

(Use foil for 'writing paper' and parsley butter instead of the *Maître d'Hôtel* sauce.)

# Fillets of Whitings

*An Eliza Acton recipe* Empty and wash thoroughly, but do not skin the fish. Take off the flesh on both sides close to the bones, passing the knife from the tail to the head; divide each side in two, trim the fillets into good shape, and fold them in a cloth, that the moisture may be well absorbed from them; dip them into, or draw them through, some beaten egg, then dip them into fine crumbs mixed with a small portion of flour, and fry them a fine light brown in lard or clarified butter; drain them well, press them in white blotting-paper, dish them one over the other in a circle, and send the usual sauce to table with them. The fillets may also be broiled after being dipped into eggs seasoned with salt and pepper, then into crumbs of bread, next into clarified butter, and a second time into the bread-crumbs (or, to shorten the process, a portion of clarified butter may be mixed with the eggs at first), and served with good melted butter, or thickened veal gravy seasoned with cayenne, lemon juice, and chopped parsley.

Five minutes will fry the fillets, even when very large; rather more time will be required to broil them.

(Whiting was very popular for breakfast in Edwardian days. This recipe is far less troublesome to eat than that where the whiting's tail is bent round and stuck into its eye cavities: there are less bones to contend with. For breakfast serve with lemon wedges and crisp fried parsley.)

# Soles Stewed in Cream

*An Eliza Acton recipe* Prepare some very fresh middling sized soles with exceeding nicety, put them into boiling water slightly salted, and simmer them for two minutes only; lift them out, and let them drain; lay them into a wide stewpan with as much sweet rich cream as will nearly cover them; add a good seasoning of pounded mace, cayenne, and salt; stew the fish softly from six to ten minutes, or until the flesh parts readily from the bones. Dish them, stir the juice of half a lemon to the sauce, pour it over the soles, and send them immediately to table. Some lemon rind may be boiled in the cream, if approved; and a small teaspoonful of arrow-root, very smoothly mixed with a little milk, may be stirred to the sauce (should it require thickening) before the lemon juice is added. Turbot and brill also may be dressed by this receipt, time proportioned to their size being of course allowed for them.

Soles, 3 or 4; boiled in water 2 minutes. Cream, $\frac{1}{2}$ to whole pint; salt, mace, cayenne; fish stewed 6 to 10 minutes. Juice of half a lemon.

(This dish is quite excellent and doesn't appear in later English cookery books. It is an eighteenth century recipe. Louisa Trotter thickened her sauce with an egg-yolk beaten with a spoonful of cream. She also filleted them after the first boiling before 'stewing' in the cream.)

## Smoked Haddock Soufflés

### Ingredients

| | |
|---|---|
| 10 ozs. cooked smoked haddock | Anchovy essence |
| 1 oz. butter | Cayenne |
| 2 eggs | 8 or 9 china or paper soufflé cases |
| Clarified butter | |

### Method

Coat the soufflé cases thickly with butter. Pound the fish whilst warm, adding the yolks of the eggs one at a time and the butter gradually, season highly with cayenne pepper, and when perfectly smooth pass through a fine sieve.

Whisk the whites of egg to a stiff froth, stir them lightly into the mixture, fill the cases three-quarters full, and bake in a quick oven for about 10 minutes.

# Afternoon Tea

## Victorian Cucumber Sandwiches

### Ingredients

Cucumber
Salad oil

*Creamed Butter:*
2 ozs. softened butter
1 tablespoon thick cream

Lemon juice
Salt and pepper

Tip of teaspoon made
  mustard
1 teaspoon lemon juice

Salt and pepper

### Method

The cucumber must be cut as thinly as possible — ideally
using a mandoline. Very lightly salt the slices and leave them
to drain in a colander lightly weighted with a plate for 2 hours

or so, pressing from time to time to get rid of excess juices.

Now dress the sliced and drained cucumber with a little oil, lemon juice, and a dredge of freshly ground white pepper (no more salt). Make up the creamed butter by blending all the ingredients together. Butter thin slices of white or brown bread; fill in the usual way, but at the last possible moment — as there is a tendency for this sandwich to be the one to give our whole repertory of sandwiches the reputation of being 'soggy'.

# Smoked Haddock Sandwiches

## Ingredients

6 ozs. cooked smoked
   haddock

Thick cream
Cayenne pepper

*Watercress Butter:*
   2 ozs. softened butter

Watercress leaves (about
   half a bunch)

Salt and pepper

## Method

Pick off all the leaves of the watercress; chop very finely, then pound with the butter in a mortar (or in a blender). Season well. Flake the haddock and mash with the thick cream, taking care the mixture isn't too sloppy.

Season with a modicum of cayenne. Make up the sandwiches in the usual way.

# Mock Caviare Sandwiches

## Ingredients

Lumpfish roe                    Lemon juice
Rye bread

*Creamed Butter:*               Thick cream
Soft butter                     Salt and pepper

## Method

Soften the butter and beat in the cream. Spread the thinnest possible slice of rye bread with the creamy butter. Spread a good layer of lumpfish roe on top, season lightly with lemon juice (no further salt will be necessary as the roe is already salty enough). Trim off all the crusts, wrap the sandwiches in a clean linen napkin, and chill well in the refrigerator before serving. (The cream prevents the butter from hardening when chilled.)

# Queen Adelaide's Sandwiches

## Ingredients

Bind equal proportions of minced chicken and ham with a little thick cream; lightly season with salt and pepper.

*Curry Butter:*                 1 teaspoon lemon
2 ozs. softened butter            juice
1 teaspoon mild curry           1 teaspoon apricot jam,
    powder or paste               sieved

# Method

Blend these ingredients together and mix to a smooth paste.

Butter thin slices of bread with the curry butter, spread a good layer of minced chicken and ham, place the top slice in position, trim off the crusts, and cut the sandwiches into fingers.

Arrange on a crisply laundered napkin, and garnish with bunches of freshly washed lightly salted watercress.

---

# Fruit Tea-Cake

## Ingredients

¾ lb. plain white flour
½ teaspoon salt
3 ozs. butter

1 oz. white sugar
2 to 3 ozs. mixed fruit
¼ pint milk
1 oz. fresh yeast

## Method

Sieve the flour and salt into a warmed bowl. Rub the butter in to the flour until the mixture resembles fine breadcrumbs. Stir in the fruit and sugar.

Heat the milk in a small saucepan to lukewarm.

In a bowl, cream the yeast with 4 tablespoons lukewarm water, and add to the flour mixture with the remaining warmed milk. Mix to a dough, turn out onto a lightly floured surface, and knead for 10 minutes or until the dough is smooth and elastic. Replace it in the bowl, and cover with a damp, folded cloth. Leave in a warm place to rise until doubled in bulk. Turn out and knead lightly. The dough can now either be shaped into 8 individual tea-cakes, or left as a single large one. Form into the shapes desired, and arrange on greased baking sheets well spaced apart. Mark the single large tea-cake into 8 wedges using a sharp knife. Cover again with a damp cloth, and leave in a warm place for 30 minutes to 1 hour, or until just about double in size.

Bake at 425°F/Mark 7, 10 to 15 minutes for the individual tea-cakes or 30 minutes for the large one. About 5 minutes before the end of the cooking time, the tea-cakes can be brushed with a sugar glaze made by heating 4 tablespoons milk with 1½ ozs. white sugar together until boiling.

Cool the tea-cakes on a wire rack and serve split and buttered. Any left over, or not quite so fresh, slice and toast and serve hot, dripping with butter.

*Note* If using dried yeast, you will need 1 tablespoonful (or ½ oz.). Dissolve this in the 4 tablespoons *hand-hot* water, and leave for 10 minutes to froth before adding to the rest of the ingredients.

# Celery Sandwiches

## Ingredients

Very finely shredded or grated celery

Salt, pepper, and squeeze of lemon juice

Thick cream to bind

*Walnut Butter:*
2 ozs. softened butter

1 oz. finely crushed walnuts

Pinch salt, pepper, cinnamon and sugar

## Method

Bind the celery with the cream; blend the ingredients together for the walnut butter.

These sandwiches are extra good when made with brown bread, 'Harvo' or 'currant bun loaf'.

Simply spread the butter, cover with a thickish cushion of the celery mixture, trim, and cut the sandwiches.

# Queen Alexandra's Sandwiches

## Ingredients

Minced cooked chicken          Mayonnaise to bind

Thin slices of tongue

*Mustard Butter*          1 teaspoon made English
2 ozs. softened butter          mustard or Moutarde
Salt and pepper          de Meaux

## Method

Butter thin slices of brown or rye bread with the mustard butter. Lay on slices of tongue; spread with the minced chicken mixture. Lay on a thickish cushion of washed and picked mustard and cress.

Trim off the crusts, cut into squares.

# Mrs Beeton's Madeira Cake

## Ingredients

1 lb. butter          The grated rind of
1½ lbs. flour          one lemon
¾ lb. castor sugar          2 thin slices of candied
Milk          peel

3 to 4 eggs

## Method

Put the butter and sugar into a clean pan (bowl), add the grated rind of one lemon, and with the hand beat it up to a very light cream; add the eggs one at a time, and beat well after each addition; then add a little milk. When all are in and the batter is very light and creamy, add the flour, stir it in lightly with the hand, and when well mixed divide the mixture equally into 3 or 4 round tins, papered at the bottoms and sides with greased white paper; dust sugar over from a dredger, and lay two very thin slices of citron peel on top. Bake in a moderate oven. They will take from 1 to $1\frac{1}{4}$ hours to bake.

*Time* 1 to $1\frac{1}{2}$ hours.

*Sufficient* for 3 or 4 medium-sized cakes.

(This is better for making as one or two larger cakes; in which case increase the baking time to $1\frac{3}{4}$ hours.)

# A Good Madeira Cake

*An Eliza Acton recipe* Whisk four fresh eggs until they are as light as possible, then, continuing still to whisk them, throw in by *slow* degrees the following ingredients in the order in which they are written: six ounces of dry, pounded, and sifted sugar; six of flour, also dried and sifted; four ounces butter just dissolved, but not heated; the rind of a fresh lemon; and the instant before the cake is moulded, beat well in the third of a teaspoonful of carbonate of soda. Bake it an hour in a moderate oven. In this, as in all compositions of the same nature, observe particularly that each portion of butter must be beaten into the mixture until no appearance of it remains before the next is added; and if this be done, and the preparation be kept light by constant and light whisking, the cake will be as good, if not better, than if the butter were creamed. Candied citron can be added to the paste, but it is not needed.

Eggs, 4; sugar, 6 oz; flour, 6 oz; butter, 4 oz; rind of one lemon; carbonate of soda, one-third of teaspoonful; 1 hour, moderate oven.

I think Miss Eliza Acton is the best person to decide what's a good Madeira Cake and what isn't; her being born in the century when this cake was used as it should be — alongside a good glass of Malmsey or Sercial Madeira; and eaten on your morning social visits.

# Genoa Cake

## Ingredients

12 ozs. flour
6 ozs. butter
6 ozs. sugar (castor)
3 eggs
About 2 tablespoonsful
  of milk or cream

The grated rind of one
  lemon
4 ozs. sultanas or
  currants
2 ozs. glacé cherries
2 ozs. almonds

## Method

Put the butter into a mixing basin, and cream it thoroughly with a wooden spoon, then add the sugar and beat well. Next stir in the eggs, previously well beaten, and add the milk or cream alternately with the sifted flour, and continue to beat the mixture well. Add the fruit, picked and cleaned, cherries, cut up, also the grated lemon rind and the almonds, blanched and cut in shreds. Mix well and put all into a cake tin, previously lined with greased paper. Bake in a moderately heated oven for about 1½ hours.

# Cherry Cake

## Ingredients

12 ozs. flour

1 teaspoonful of

8 ozs. butter
6 ozs. castor sugar
4 ozs. glacé cherries
2 or 3 eggs

baking powder
The grated rind of one
  lemon
Milk

## Method

Line a cake tin with greased paper, sieve the flour and the baking powder together, and grate the lemon rind into it. Cream the butter and sugar, add the eggs, which should be well beaten, stir in the flour lightly, and the cherries cut into halves and, if necessary, a little milk: but keep the mixture fairly stiff. Bake in a moderate oven.

*Time* to bake, $1\frac{1}{2}$ hours.

*Sufficient* for one cake.

# Sponge Cake

## Ingredients

8 eggs
Their weight in
  castor sugar

The weight of 5 eggs
  in flour
The rind of 1 lemon

## Method

Put the eggs into one side of the scale, and take the weight of 8 in castor sugar, and the weight of 5 in good *dry* flour. Separate the yolks from the whites of the eggs; beat the former, put them into a saucepan with the sugar, and let them remain over the fire until *milk-warm*, keeping them well stirred. Then put them into a basin, add the grated lemon rind, and beat these ingredients well together. Whisk the whites of the eggs to a stiff froth, stir them into the other ingredients, and beat the cake well for $\frac{1}{4}$ hour. Then take out the whisk, sieve in the flour, and whisk it lightly with a wooden spoon. Put it into a greased (use clarified butter) mould, dusted out with a little finely sifted sugar and flour, and bake the cake in a quick oven for $1\frac{1}{2}$ hours. Care must be taken that it is put into the oven immediately, or it will not be light. The flavouring of this cake may be varied by adding a few drops of essence of almonds, instead of the grated lemon rind.

*Time* $1\frac{1}{2}$ hours.

*Sufficient* for one cake.

# Rice Cake

## Ingredients

| | |
|---|---|
| $\frac{1}{2}$ lb. ground rice | A few drops of essence |
| $\frac{1}{2}$ lb. flour | of lemon, or the grated |
| 6 ozs. castor sugar | rind of half a lemon |
| 3 or 4 eggs | $\frac{1}{2}$ lb. butter or margarine |
| | Milk |

## Method

Sieve the rice and flour together onto a sheet of paper. Put the butter and sugar into a clean basin, add the yellow rind of the lemon grated, and beat to a cream. Add the eggs one at a time, and when all are in add the flour, moisten to cake-batter consistency, using a little milk if necessary. Turn into one or two greased moulds, and bake in a moderate oven from 1 to 2 hours.

If preferred, the cake may be flavoured with essence of almonds.

*Time* about $1\frac{1}{2}$ hours.

*Sufficient* for 2 medium-sized cakes.

(Often copper and tin moulds were used for this type of cake. The finished cake was dredged with icing sugar before serving.)

# Saffron Cake

## Ingredients

2 lbs. flour
½ oz. yeast
1 lb. butter
4 eggs

¼ lb. currants
½ lb. sugar
¼ of a drachm (a pinch or two) of saffron
¼ lb. Malaga raisins

## Method

Dissolve the yeast in ½ pint of tepid water, put it into a clean basin, and stir in sufficient flour to make a nice soft dough. Well knead it, and leave it in the basin covered over in a warm place to prove. When well proved, take the remaining flour, turn it out onto the board, make a bay in the centre, put in the butter and sugar, and rub these together till smooth; then add the eggs and piece of fermented dough, and mix all well up together, mixing in the whole of the flour, and adding the saffron liquor which has been previously infused in a ¼ pint of warm water and strained. Well and thoroughly mix by rubbing it on the board, then add the raisins stoned and cut up, and the currants previously cleaned; then turn it into a large well greased mould, or two smaller ones, stand it aside to prove and, when well proved, bake in a moderate oven from 1½ to 2 hours.

*Time* 1½ to 2 hours to bake.
*Sufficient* for one large cake.

(Saffron of this type — powder — comes in miniature thimbles and is obtainable from most good grocers.)

# Sand Cake

## Ingredients

½ lb. cornflour
1 oz. rice flour
   (or ground rice)

6 ozs. butter
6 ozs. castor sugar
2 eggs
A little icing sugar

## Method

Sieve the two flours together, beat the butter and sugar until quite white and creamy. Break in each egg separately and beat very well, then carefully stir in the flours. Grease a tin mould and dust with flour, or some finely-powdered Savoy cake; put in the mixture and bake in a moderate oven. When cold dredge with icing sugar.
*Time* about 1 hour.
*Sufficient* for one cake.

# Acton Gingerbread

A lot of people down here in London get this mixed up with 'Parkin' — like what Johnny's cook makes, up at his Yorkshire place; but that has oatmeal in it and sticks to the roof of your mouth; not that it isn't good, mind you (there's a receipt for it on page 162), but you mustn't get things muddled up.

This is a posh recipe like most of Miss Acton's are; her being eighteenth-century minded, if you understand what I mean. We always serve it for tea at the Bentinck in the winter. You can't make enough of it for those Eton and Harrow lads and their Dads too!

Whisk four strained or well-cleared eggs to the lightest possible froth and put to them, by degrees, a pound and a quarter of treacle, still beating them lightly. Add, in the same manner, six ounces of pale brown sugar free from lumps, one pound of sifted flour, and six ounces of good butter, *just* sufficiently warmed to be liquid, and no more, for if hot, it would render the cake heavy; it should be poured in small portions to the mixture, which should be well beaten up with the back of a wooden spoon as each portion is thrown in: the success of the cake depends almost entirely on this part of the process. When properly mingled with the mass, the butter will not be perceptible on the surface; and if the cake be kept light by constant whisking, large bubbles will appear in it to the last. When it is so far ready, add to it one ounce of Jamaica ginger and a large teaspoonful of cloves in fine powder, with the lightly grated rinds of two fresh full-sized lemons. Butter thickly, in every part, a shallow square tin pan, and bake the gingerbread slowly for nearly or quite an hour in a gentle oven. Let it cool a little before it is turned out, and set it on its edge until cold, supporting it, if needful, against a large jar or bowl. We have usually had it baked in an American oven, in a tin less than two inches deep; and it has been excellent. We retain the name given to it originally in our own circle.

# Yorkshire Parkin

## Ingredients

4 lbs. fine oatmeal
3 lbs. treacle or
  golden syrup
6 ozs. butter or lard

¼ lb. brown moist
  sugar
1 oz. ground ginger
Milk

## Method

Let the treacle warm gradually by the side of the fire until it becomes quite liquid. Rub the butter or lard into the oatmeal, add the sugar and ginger, and stir in the treacle with a wooden spoon. The vessel which held the treacle should be rinsed out with beer, but milk may be substituted; this is added gradually until the right consistency is obtained. The mixture must be smooth, but not drop too easily from the spoon. Have ready some greased Yorkshire pudding tins, pour in the mixture, and bake in a steady oven until the centre of the parkin feels firm. As the mixture improves by being allowed to stand, each cake should be baked separately when the oven is a small one. Let the parkin cool slightly, then cut it into squares, remove them from the tin, and when cold place them in an airtight biscuit tin. The parkin may be kept for months (in fact it is improved by doing so).

*Time* to bake, from 1 to 1½ hours.
*Sufficient* for 2 or 3 cakes.

---

# Pikelets

---

## Ingredients

1 lb. plain white flour
1 teaspoon salt
1 pint milk

1 teaspoon castor sugar
¼ teaspoon bicarbonate
of soda

½ oz. fresh yeast

## Method

Sift the flour and salt into a large, warmed bowl. Heat the milk and sugar to lukewarm in a small saucepan. Transfer about 3 tablespoons of the liquid to a bowl, and cream in the yeast. Make a 'well' in the centre of the flour and gradually pour in the creamed yeast and warmed milk, beating to a smooth batter. Beat, using your hand, for a good 5 minutes, then cover with a damp, folded cloth, and leave aside in a warm place for about 45 minutes to 1 hour.

Dissolve the bicarbonate of soda in 4 tablespoons of warm water. Beat this into the dough, and leave to rise for a further 1 hour.

Grease a griddle and the pikelet rings. Heat the rings on the griddle and half-fill them with spoonsful of the mixture. Allow to cook for 4 to 5 minutes, then turn them over and finish cooking on the other side. Ease off the rings and leave them to cool before greasing and using for the next batch. Toast the pikelets and serve piping hot spread generously with butter.

*Note* If using dried yeast, you will need 1½ teaspoonsful (or ¼ oz.). Dissolve this in ¼ pint of the hand-hot milk and sugar, and leave for 10 minutes to froth before adding to the flour.

---

# Muffins

## Ingredients

| | |
|---|---|
| ½ pint milk | 1 teaspoon castor sugar |
| ½ oz. fresh yeast | 1 lb. plain white flour |
| 1 teaspoon salt | 1 egg, beaten |

## Method

Heat the milk and sugar together in a saucepan to lukewarm. Transfer about 3 tablespoons of the liquid to a bowl, and cream in the yeast.

Sift the flour and salt into a large, warmed bowl and rub in the butter. Make a 'well' in the centre, and pour in the warmed milk, creamed yeast, and beaten egg. Mix to a dough, adding more flour or warm water if necessary to obtain a soft but not sticky dough. Turn out onto a lightly floured work-surface, and knead until smooth and elastic — about 10 minutes. Replace the dough in the bowl, cover with a damp, folded cloth, and leave in a warm place until doubled in bulk — about 45 minutes to 1 hour.

Turn out the dough, knead lightly, and roll out to $\frac{1}{2}$ inch thick. Use a floured, plain 3 inch cutter to cut out the rounds. Re-roll any trimmings, and cut out the remaining muffins — you should get about 12 in all.

Flour some baking sheets and place the muffins on them. Sprinkle the muffins with flour, and then leave in a warm place to rise for a further 30 minutes, or until the muffins look puffy. Place the muffins, a few at a time, on a warmed, lightly greased griddle. Cook over a low heat for 6 to 8 minutes on each side. Pull them apart and put large lumps of butter inside. Keep warm whilst cooking the rest.

After a few days, any remaining muffins can be sliced and served toasted and buttered.

*Note* If using dried yeast, you will need 2 teaspoonsful. Dissolve this in half the warmed liquid, and leave 10 minutes to froth before adding to the flour with the remaining liquid.

# Sultana Scones

## Ingredients

1 lb. white or brown flour
$\frac{3}{4}$ teaspoon cream of tartar
2 ozs. lard
4 ozs. sultanas
Buttermilk, sour milk, or milk

$\frac{3}{4}$ teaspoon bicarbonate of soda
2 ozs. unsalted butter
2 ozs. castor sugar
2 eggs

## Method

Sift flour with bicarbonate and cream of tartar. Rub in the two fats. Toss in sugar and fruit. Beat eggs with a little milk; mix with dry ingredients until a soft dough. Knead very lightly. Press out into a $\frac{3}{4}$ inch thick sheet, cut into squares, triangles, or circles.

Bake in moderate oven (Gas 6, Elec. 400°) for 10 to 15 minutes. Or bake on a griddle.

# Lemon Biscuits

## Ingredients

¾ lb. flour
3 ozs. fresh butter
The grated rind of a
    lemon

6 ozs. castor sugar
2 eggs
1 dessertspoonful of lemon
    juice

## Method

Rub the butter into the flour, stir in the castor sugar and very finely-minced lemon peel, and when these ingredients are thoroughly mixed, add the eggs, which should be previously well whisked, and the lemon juice.

Beat the mixture well for 1 or 2 minutes, then drop it from a spoon on to a greased tin, about 2 inches apart, as the biscuits will spread when they get warm. Place the tin in the oven, and bake the biscuits a pale brown from 15 to 20 minutes.

# Digestive Biscuits

## Ingredients

6 ozs. wholemeal flour
½ teaspoon salt
3 ozs. butter
1 teaspoon baking powder

1 oz. oatmeal
1 oz. white flour
Sugar to taste
Enough milk to bind

166

## Method

Rub fat into the dry ingredients and add just enough milk to bind. Knead. Roll out thinly, cut, prick, and bake in a moderate oven. (Do not overbake.)

# Brandy Snaps

## Ingredients

¼ lb. flour  
¼ lb. sugar  
¼ oz. ginger  

¼ lb. butter  
¼ lb. syrup  
Juice of half a lemon  

Lemon-flavoured whipped cream

## Method

Melt sugar, butter and syrup, add the warmed flour, ginger and lemon. Stir well and put out on a well-greased baking-sheet in teaspoonful, 6 inches apart. Bake in a moderate oven until golden brown, leave for a few moments to cool, then roll up over the thick handle of a wooden spoon and fill with lemon-flavoured whipped cream.

# Shortbread

## Ingredients

4 ozs. unsalted butter  
4 ozs. white flour ⎫ mixed  
2 ozs. ground rice ⎭ together  

2 ozs. castor sugar  
Split almonds or candied peel  

Extra castor sugar

## Method

Cream butter and sugar; gradually add flours; pat out into a circle ¼ inch to an inch thick. Place on buttered baking sheet; prick all over with a fork; shape the edges with finger and thumb.

Mark into wedges with a knife (making a circle in the middle with a tin cutter or glass). Dredge with almonds and castor sugar *or* decorate with pieces of peel.

Bake in moderate oven for 30 minutes, or until pale biscuit colour.

# Scotch Shortbread

## Ingredients

2 lbs. flour
1 lb. butter (unsalted)
¼ lb. castor sugar

¼ lb. cornflour or ground
rice
1 oz. sweet almonds

A few strips of candied orange-peel

## Method

Beat the butter to a cream, add gradually the flour, sugar, and sweet almonds, blanched and shredded. Knead until it is quite smooth, divide into 6 pieces, each cake on a separate piece of paper (rice-paper), roll out square to the thickness of 1 inch, and pinch round the edges. Prick well with a skewer, ornament with 1 or 2 strips of candied orange-peel, and bake in a moderately hot oven from 25 to 30 minutes.

*Time* 25 to 30 minutes.

*Sufficient* to make 6 cakes.

# Almond Macaroons

*An Eliza Acton recipe* Blanch a pound of fresh Jordan almonds, wipe them dry, and set them into a very cool oven to render them perfectly so; pound them to an exceedingly smooth paste, with a little white of egg, then whisk to a firm solid froth the white of seven eggs, or of eight, should they be small, mix with them a pound and a half of the finest sugar; add these by degrees to the almonds, whisk the whole up well together, and drop the mixture upon wafer-paper, which may be procured at the confectioner's; bake the cakes in a moderate oven to a very pale brown. It is an improvement to their flavour to substitute an ounce with an equal weight of each; and another variety of them is obtained by gently browning the almonds in a slow oven before they are pounded.

Jordan almonds blanched, 1 lb. (or 1 lb. ground almonds); sugar, 1½ lbs.; whites of 7 or 8 eggs: 15 to 20 minutes.

*Note* Until I got 'Frenchified' I used to get Mrs Wellkin to make these up for them to eat with their coffee after dinner. She's improved them a bit, by baking them on rice paper and topping each one with a whole blanched almond; a bit extravagant, I suppose, but then I'm like that, aren't I?

You can put glacé cherries on some if you like and a bit of angelica cut like a diamond on others: makes them pretty, which is what I like.

# My Wedding Cake

It was one morning when I was in bed with the 'flu that Mrs Catchpole (Lord Henry's housekeeper) came into my room telling me I ought to get married.

'You can't be a cook — I mean you can't go *out* to cook, for *important* people that is . . . unless you're married.'

And I believed her, mainly because I knew that all cooks and housekeepers were known as Mrs This or That. I didn't twig just at that time what was going on behind my back — a right conspiracy, I can tell you — Lord Henry, Mrs Catchpole, Major Farjeon all getting their heads together to get me lined up for His Royal Highness.

Well, you all know what happened, but I was mad at the time: I mean, how dare they push me around like a sack of coal, just to please their little whims and fancies!

Gus — Augustus, that is — finally convinced me that we ought to play their game, but even he thought he could get away with it easy.

'I'll go straight round to the Registrar's Office,' he said, but

I told him flat, 'If I'm going to get married at all, I'm going to get married proper!'

So we decided to do it at St. Saviour's, Pimlico — a nice little church, and just round the corner, handy like.

Not having that much money to throw around, I decided to wear a white frock which I already had. Mary wasn't much impressed but, as I told her, 'It's white, and good enough for a wedding dress.'

Lord Henry was very kind and sent champagne down to the kitchen for us to have with the wedding tea. There was my Mum and Dad, Mrs Catchpole, Mary, Ivy, a few of me friends, and, of course, Monsieur Alex. He proposed a toast to me and Gus — one of the nicest speeches it was. 'She is a Princess of the culinary arts. Born with a rare and delicate touch for a cabbage, for a chicken, for what you will . . . She can, if she wishes, become *une reine de la cuisine* . . .' Fair made me swallow hard, it did.

He then sends Ivy into his pantry, and she staggers back with a beautiful wedding cake — all very fancy and prettied-up. Bless his heart: he'd made a real copy of Mrs Beeton's wedding cake! You see, the French don't go in for the same sort of rich, dark fruit cake like what we do. I've used that same recipe ever since whenever I've had to bake a good rich cake: mind you, I've given it a face-lift and added my own ideas, but it's worth a try any day, and the decorations are easy-made, if you follow my instructions. It was never very fashionable even in the old girl's days (Queen Victoria) to have real flowers on your wedding cake, because brides like to keep the topknot for a keepsake: so I've kept up with Monsieur Alex's idea and I still use beautiful artificial flowers and ribbons and suchlike.

172

# The Wedding Cake

## Ingredients

8 ozs. plain flour
Grated rind and juice of a
  lemon and an orange
4 ozs. ground almonds (your
  own grinding)
4 ozs. chopped glacé cherries
12 ozs. sultanas
4 ozs. chopped French
  candied peel
3 large eggs
Glass of dark rum

Level teaspoon each of:
  ground nutmeg
  ginger
  cloves
  cinnamon
12 ozs. currants
8 ozs. seedless raisins
8 ozs. unsalted butter
8 ozs. soft brown sugar
$\frac{1}{2}$ pint Madeira wine
2 ozs. syrup

Tablespoon orange flower water

## Method

Line a cake tin (about a 6 lb. tin or two 3 lb. tins) with treble thickness of buttered greaseproof paper — sides and bottom. The side papers coming some 2 inches above the rim of the tin. Tie firmly with string. Stand the tin on a baking sheet.

Cream the butter and sugar until all the granules are dissolved. Mix flour and spices together; mix in dried fruits which have been well picked and cleaned. Beat eggs together with the rum, Madeira, flower water and fruit juices with their grated rinds; warm syrup and mix together with the egg mixture. Make a well in the fruit and flour mixture and gradually incorporate the egg mixture, gathering the dry ingredients in as you go along.

Fill the tin two-thirds full. Level off the top of the mixture with a palette knife.

Bake at Gas 3, Elec. 325° for an hour; reduce the heat to Gas 2 Elec. 300° for a further hour or until the cake is 'silent' and a skewer when plunged into the centre comes away clean.

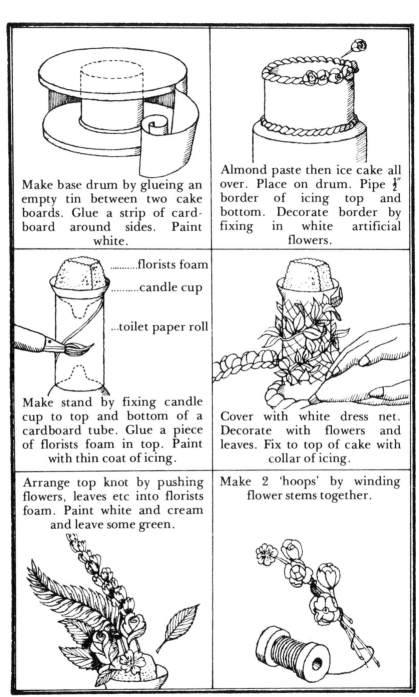

Make base drum by glueing an empty tin between two cake boards. Glue a strip of cardboard around sides. Paint white.

Almond paste then ice cake all over. Place on drum. Pipe $\frac{1}{2}''$ border of icing top and bottom. Decorate border by fixing in white artificial flowers.

..........florists foam

..........candle cup

...toilet paper roll

Make stand by fixing candle cup to top and bottom of a cardboard tube. Glue a piece of florists foam in top. Paint with thin coat of icing.

Cover with white dress net. Decorate with flowers and leaves. Fix to top of cake with collar of icing.

Arrange top knot by pushing flowers, leaves etc into florists foam. Paint white and cream and leave some green.

Make 2 'hoops' by winding flower stems together.

How to decorate Louisa Trotter's Wedding Cake.

174

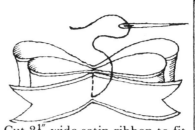

| | |
|---|---|
| Push hoops into the foam and bend round to touch rim of cake. | Cut 2½" wide satin ribbon to fit all round base drum. Make up bow separately. Sew on side, stitching on posy of flowers. Decorate rest of cake with more flowers, at will. |

The cake is better for keeping 2 or 3 weeks before covering first with the almond paste and then allowing that to dry out somewhat over 2 or 3 days. Finally coat with Royal Icing then decorate as shown.

# Almond Paste

## Ingredients

To 1 lb. of castor sugar allow ¾ lb. of ground sweet almonds, 2 or 3 eggs, a little rose or orange-flower water.

## Method

Weigh the castor sugar and ground almonds into a clean basin, and mix them well together; make a hole in the centre, break in the 2 eggs, add a little rose water, and wet up into a firm paste, using another egg if necessary. Turn the mixture out of the pan on to the board, dusting it over with sugar to prevent it from sticking, then roll it out with a rolling-pin to the size of the cake, place it on top and press smooth with the hand.

*Time* ¾ hour.

*Sufficient* for a cake weighing from 2 to 3 lbs.

(This paste needs well beating with a sugared rolling pin; it is good and rich but 'oils' readily. Roll out the paste on a board and invert the cake onto this; pressing the edges smooth and 'running it off' down the sides of the cake. When turned right way up, the cake will have a flat top when covered with almond paste in this way.)

# Royal Icing

## Ingredients

1½ lb. confectioner's icing sugar, finely sieved

The whites of 3 or 4 eggs
The juice of 1 lemon

## Method

Icing sugar can now be obtained from almost every grocery store, or failing that, a pastry cook would supply the quantity required. Having procured the sugar, take a very clean basin and spoon, turn in the sugar, and carefully break in the whites of the eggs; add a small pinch of blue, and then proceed to beat up the icing. When well beaten and smooth add the strained juice of 1 lemon, then beat it up thoroughly until it will stand up in the pan. Now take the cake and set it on an inverted plate, or if you have it, a regular turn-table used by confectioners for the purpose. Take up, with a spoon, sufficient icing to cover the top, and lay it upon the centre of the cake. Now take a large pliable palette-knife and spread the icing level on top. Then take up small portions of the icing with the point of the palette knife, spread it smoothly round the side, and when the cake is completely enveloped, stand it

176

aside in a warm place to dry. During the time the cake is drying and as soon as it is hard enough, a thin sheet of paper should be lightly laid right over the top to prevent the dust from spoiling the colour of the cake.

*Time* 30 minutes to make.

*Sufficient* for one cake.

(To aid the spreading of the icing use a palette knife, 6 inch size, frequently dipped into a jug of boiling water.)

## Sweets, Puddings & Ice-Cream

## Oranges filled with Jelly

*An Eliza Acton recipe* This is one of the fanciful dishes which make a pretty appearance on a supper table, and are acceptable when much variety is desired. Take some very fine oranges, and with the point of a small knife cut out from the top of each, a round about the size of a shilling; then with the small end of a tea or an egg spoon, empty them entirely, taking great care not to break the rinds. Throw these into cold water, and make jelly of the juice, which must be well pressed from the pulp, and strained as clear as possible. Colour one half a fine rose colour with prepared cochineal, and leave the other very pale; when it is nearly cold, drain and wipe the orange-rinds, and fill them with alternate stripes of the two jellies; when they are perfectly cold cut them into quarters, and dispose them tastefully in a dish with a few light branches of myrtle between them. Calf's feet or any other variety of jelly, or different blancmanges, may be used at choice to fill the rinds; the colours, however, should contrast as much as possible.

# Prince of Wales' Pudding

Created at the Bentinck for H.M. (Edward VII) when Prince of Wales.

## Ingredients

*Base* 1 fatless sponge cake
  (8 inches diameter)
4 oranges, segmented

Orange sorbet or vanilla
  ice cream (8 portions)
Icing sugar

*Orange Sauce* ½ pint orange
  juice
2 ozs. castor sugar

1 teaspoon finely shredded
  orange rind
Potato flour (see Method)

2 tablespoons Kirsch

## Method

First make the orange sauce. Remove the rind from those oranges in the first part of this recipe, using a potato peeler. Take care not to take off any of the white pith as this is bitter. Now shred this as fine as thread with a sharp knife. (If you are not adept at fine-shredding, lightly grate the rind from the orange.)

Put this peel together with the sugar and juice into a pan and bring to the boil. Slake about a teaspoon of potato flour in a little cold water, and stir this a little at a time into the boiling liquid. It will thicken immediately. Stop adding the potato flour as soon as the sauce has good viscous consistency.

Add the Kirsch. Sprinkle the surface of the sauce with a little extra castor sugar to prevent a skin from forming, and stand the pan in a second pan of hot water to keep hot whilst you make the basic 'pudding'.

Split the cake in half 'equatorwise'. Scoop out some of the crumbs and dredge the top layer with plenty of icing sugar. Stand the base on a serving dish — test that the whole affair is going to fit under your grill comfortably. Arrange the orange segments on the base, scoop over the ice-cream or sorbet.

Fit the lid and set under a spanking hot grill, allowing the sugar to caramelise. Serve immediately with the hot sauce.

If you don't have adequate space to fit the whole affair under the grill, just put the top under to caramelise before sitting it atop the ice-cream.

# Crème Caramel

The quality of this delicious pudding can be varied by adding more egg yolks and by using half single cream and half milk:

## Ingredients

*Custard*

4 whole eggs ⎱ or 5
2 egg yolks ⎰ eggs

2 ozs. castor cugar
½ pint milk ⎱ or 1 pint milk
½ pint single cream ⎰

2 pieces lemon rind or piece (2 inches) vanilla pod,
or 1 teaspoon vanilla essence

*Caramel* 4 ozs. castor sugar    4 tablespoons water

## Method

Select a ring mould or ovenproof dish large enough to contain the mixture (about 1½ pints). Line this with caramel as instructed below:

Beat eggs, yolks and sugar together until fluffy. Slowly bring to the boil milk and cream, or just milk, with lemon essence or vanilla pod. Pour the boiling milk onto the egg mixture, whisking with a balloon whisk all the time. Strain the egg and milk mixture into the lined mould. Stand this in another tin of hot water, and bake on the centre shelf of *pre-heated* oven for 45 minutes, or until set and firm to the touch. (Gas 3, Elec. 325°.)

*To line the mould* Put the sugar and water into a small pan, and slowly bring to the boil, stirring until all the sugar has dissolved. Then over a medium heat — don't stir again or it will crystallise — allow the caramel to take a good deep colour. Have two cloths ready to hold the mould, pour the hot caramel into this, and swirl it round until the sides are well-coated. This will take a minute or two, and the dish will get very hot! If the caramel is too 'heavy', dip the mould into boiling water and it will loosen up so that you can successfully coat it. *Do not* be tempted to dip your fingers into the caramel or you will get a nasty burn.

*Notes on Crème Caramel* Have a bowl of cold water at the ready so that when the caramel is of a good deep colour you can dip the bottom of the pan into this and arrest any retained heat which may just be enough to burn it. Sugar takes quite a while to get to the first pale stages of caramelising, but then tends to get into a hurry, so these little safety devices are handy.

Likewise, if it stiffens up when coating it is necessary to have a pan of boiling water at the ready. See recipe.

So that you have the smoothest of custards, don't whisk too briskly as this beats air bubbles into the mixture. It is as well to stir slowly and stir one way. Pedantic! But fact!

# Charlotte Russe

This popular Edwardian sweet is simple to make.

Make up a Bavarian Cream (p. 182), select a suitable sized Charlotte mould. Run $\frac{1}{4}$ inch of lemon jelly into the bottom and put to set. Remove the mould from the refrigerator and decorate the jelly attractively with fruit, cut into attractive shapes, or crystallised fruit.

Carefully pour over the merest film of jelly, and return the mould to the refrigerator to 'fix' the decoration. Now pour over about ½ inch more jelly and again put to set. Use boudoir biscuits or *langue de chats* to line the mould — rounded side of the biscuit to the mould wall. Fill with the Bavarian Cream mixture well-laced with your favourite liqueur (in which case reduce the quantity of milk in the preparation accordingly).

Again put to set. Turn out onto a tazza; tie an attractive bow of ribbon round the Charlotte's waist (this also helps support the walls).

# Bavarian Cream

## Ingredients

3 egg yolks

¾ pint single cream or milk

⅛ pint water

2 ozs. castor sugar

½ oz. gelatine crystals

¼ pint cream

1 inch piece vanilla pod, or teaspoon vanilla essence
(or lemon rind)

## Method

Cream egg yolks and sugar. Bring the milk to the boil with the vanilla pod; pour onto the egg mixture. Return the mixture to the pan and, over a low heat, thicken, as for a custard. Put the gelatine into a small basin, stand this in a pan of boiling water, and when it is completely melted pour into the waiting warm custard. Stir well in. (N.B. Never pour cold gelatine into a hot mixture or hot gelatine into cold.) Allow to cool, but not set.

Whip the cream until it just starts to stand in peaks (but still 'falls back'). Fold the cream into the custard. Fill into a mould or bowl, put to set in a refrigerator.

# Walnut Pie

## Ingredients

*Sweet pastry*

6 ozs. plain white flour

1 teaspoon lemon juice

1 tablespoon cold water

4 ozs. unsalted butter

2 ozs. icing sugar

1 egg

*Filling*

2 tablespoons clear honey

4 ozs. ground almonds

2 eggs

4 ozs. castor sugar

1 tablespoon lemon
juice

2 ozs. walnuts roughly chopped

## Method

Lightly rub the butter into the flour until you have a sandy texture. Sift in the sugar, incorporating this by letting it run through the fingers as you lift and 'rain' the flour and butter mixture.

Make a well in the centre of these dry ingredients, beat the egg and add the water and lemon juice to it, and pour into the well. Work the mixture quickly and deftly into a dough and leave to rest for half an hour.

Roll out two-thirds of the pastry and line an 8 inch flan ring or loose-bottomed tart tin. Roll out a lid and put on one side whilst you make the filling.

Separate the eggs. Cream the yolks with the sugar until they are white and fluffy. Beat in honey, add ground almonds. Add the roughly chopped walnuts. Stiffly beat the egg-whites and fold into the mixture, adding a tablespoon at first to 'slacken' the walnut mixture.

Fill the lined flan ring, wet the edges, add the lid, seal, and pinch or fork round the edge so that it looks attracive. Bake in the centre of a pre-heated oven at Gas 6, Electricity 400°, for 40 minutes. Dredge with a little castor sugar 10 minutes before the end of the baking time.

Remove the ring and stand the finished pie on a cooling tray. Serve with plenty of whipped cream.

*Note* This pie is also good when made with brown sugar.

# Damson Pudding

## Ingredients

Suet crust (p. 194)                1½ pints of damsons
2 tablespoonsful of brown        ½ teaspoon cinnamon
   sugar or to taste

## Method

Line the 2 pint basin with suet crust, half fill with fruit, add the sugar and cinnamon, and then the remainder of the fruit. Put on the cover, carefully seal the edges, and if the pudding is to be boiled, tie in a scalded well-floured cloth; if steamed, cover it with a sheet of greased paper (or foil). Cook from 2½ to 3 hours.

# Vanilla Blancmange

## Ingredients

¾ pint milk                        ¼ pint cream

3 ozs. loaf sugar
2 yolks of eggs

1 oz. gelatine
2 inches of vanilla pod

## Method

Bring the milk, sugar and vanilla pod to boiling point, and simmer gently until sufficiently flavoured. Beat the yolks of eggs slightly, strain onto them the boiling milk, stirring vigorously meanwhile, return to the stewpan, and stir by the side of the fire until the mixture thickens. Dissolve the gelatine in ¼ pint of water, add it to the custard and, when cool, remove the vanilla pod, stir in the stiffly-whipped cream. Stand on ice or in a cold place until set.

# Nesselrode Pudding

## Ingredients

18 chestnuts
4 egg-yolks
½ pint milk
1 vanilla pod
¼ pint pineapple syrup
3 ozs. glacé pineapple

2 ozs. diced citron peel
3 ozs. glacé cherries
2 ozs. seeded raisins
3½ fl. ozs. maraschino
½ pint whipped double
   cream

## Method

Pierce the chestnuts and then boil them. When tender remove both inner and outer skins and rub through a sieve. Place the purée in the top of a double saucepan, over hot water, with the egg yolks, milk, crushed vanilla pod and pineapple syrup and stir over a moderate heat until thick smooth custard is achieved. This is an elaborate form of basic confectioners' custard. If any lumps remain rub through a sieve into a large bowl.

In a separate heat-resistant container place the diced citron peel and the rough cut glacé pineapple. Then add the cherries, the seeded raisins and the maraschino and allow the fruit to steep under a tight covering of foil for 4 hours. Meanwhile cover the bowl of custard mixture with foil and freeze until the edges are firm and the centre is just beginning to set. Whip down and fold in the fruit in its maraschino. Blend well together and then cut in the whipped cream gently until smooth. Put into a lightly oiled mould, cover with foil and freeze until required.

To serve, hold the mould upside down under the hot tap for an instant to unmould, but do not hold for too long or the outline of the mould pattern will become blurred. Garnish with *marrons glacés.*

# Bentinck Apple Pie

## Ingredients

| | |
|---|---|
| Apples | Shortcrust pastry |
| Sugar | Water |
| Lemon rind | Cloves |

Rose petals if in season.

## Method

Wash some apples; peel and core them and throw the peelings and cores into ½ pint cold water. Let them stew for half an hour. Strain off and let the liquor get cold; halve and quarter the apples, and if they are very large cut the quarters in halves crosswise, but never cut thin slices, because if you do the juice will boil out before the apples are cooked. Pile the apples in a pie-dish, making them high in the centre, add the sugar and the grated rind of half a lemon.

When it is cold strain the liquid from the peelings and cores and pour it all over the sugar. Cover the fruit with old-fashioned cottage rose petals or a tablespoon of rose flower water.

Make a shortcrust pastry by rubbing 6 ozs. butter and 2 ozs. of pure lard into 1 lb. of good plain flour; mix in 4 tablespoons castor sugar and the yolk of an egg well beaten with about $\frac{1}{2}$ pint of cold water. Roll out $\frac{1}{4}$ inch thick. Leave the pastry on the board or slab for 10 minutes to recover.

Wet the edges of the pie-dish. Cover the pie with pastry, being careful not to stretch it. Some cooks like a strip of pastry on the rim of the pie-dish before putting on the pastry cover. If so, wet it as well as the rim. Trim the edges with a sharp knife cutting them quite straight, and do not ornament at all (the reason for this is that in the old days a number of pies both meat and fruit, would be made at the same time on baking days and the fruit ones were distinguished by not being ornamented — consequently it became the correct thing not to ornament fruit pies, but to keep them perfectly plain). As a matter of fact, they look very much nicer perfectly plain if the pastry is well made, and in baking rises and forms a good shaped dome. This is achieved by putting them first into a hot oven, and lowering the heat to finish them off in a cooler one in order to cook the fruit.

Bake in a moderate-to-hot oven (Gas 6, Elec. 400°) for 20 to 30 minutes.

When serving sift castor sugar over the top and glaze by holding a minute or two under grill.

# Quince Blancmange

## Ingredients

| | |
|---|---|
| 1 lb. ripe quinces | 6 ozs. castor sugar |
| $\frac{3}{4}$ oz. gelatine | $\frac{1}{4}$ pint double cream |
| | 1 pint water |

# Method

Peel and core the quinces, simmer them in the water until quite soft and broken, but not reduced to a pulp, then strain through a jelly-bag. Replace the liquor in the pan, add the sugar and the gelatine previously soaked in a little cold water, and stir and boil gently until the gelatine is dissolved. When cool, add the cream, mix well, and turn into a mould rinsed with cold water.

(Use pears instead of quinces adding a teaspoonful of rose flower water.)

# An Excellent Trifle

Any good cook should know how to make a good trifle, but there's many who get it wrong. Those 'I-ties' with their *Zuppa Inglese* haven't done much good to it either.

It's as easy as falling flat on your face; good custard; good sponge cake, plenty of the booze, and a topping like an 'Ascot hat'.

Try this one first, then see how me and my girls have improved it. We never get no complaints about our trifles at the Bentinck, I can tell you.

*An Eliza Acton recipe* Take equal parts of wine and brandy, about a wineglassful of each, or two-thirds of good sherry or Madeira, and one of spirit, and soak in the mixture four sponge-biscuits, and half a pound of macaroons and ratafias; cover the bottom of the trifle-dish with part of these, and pour upon them a full pint of rich boiled custard made with three-quarters of a pint, or rather more, of milk and cream taken in equal portions, and six eggs. Lay the remainder of the soaked cakes upon it, and pile over the whole, to the depth of two or three inches, a whipped syllabub, previously well drained: then sweeten and flavour slightly with wine only less than half-a-pint of cream. Wash and wipe the whisk, and whip the

188

cream to the lightest possible froth: take it off with a skimmer and heap it gently over the trifle.

Macaroons and ratafias, ½ lb.; wine and brandy mixed, ¼ pint; rich boiled custard, 1 pint; whipped syllabub; light froth to cover the whole, short ½ pint of cream; sugar, dessertspoonful; wine, ½ glassful.

# Cheese Cake

This 200-year-old recipe is far too scrumptious to be left at the bottom of any drawer. It must never be forgotten that the Georgians had more kinds of pastry than we tend to use today. Modern sweet pastry (or Pâte Frollée) was frequently used for 'pyes' which today may well be called flans, and in this recipe for cheese cake yet another name appears. It matters not what's in a name — what is more important is what goes into the making of this dish.

## Ingredients

*The pastry* 4 ozs. plain flour
2 ozs. unsalted butter

2 ozs. castor sugar
1 egg-yolk
1 tablespoon cold water
Icing sugar

*The filling* 4 eggs
6 ozs. castor sugar
Juice and grated rind of 2 lemons

1 lb. cottage cheese
½ oz. plain flour
2 ozs. flaked sweet almonds

## Method

First make the pastry. Rub the butter into the flour as lightly as possible. Dredge in the sugar. Beat the egg-yolk with water and deftly mix the paste to a loose dough. Do not over-knead

189

the pastry or it will be tough and shrink from the sides of the flan ring.

Line an 8 inch flan ring with this pastry. Put a large circle of foil (shiny side to the pastry) into the flan ring to hold the sides in place while it is baked in the oven at Gas 5, Electricity 375°, for 15 minutes. Remove the foil very carefully.

Now make the filling. Separate the eggs. Beat the yolks with the sugar until the granules are dissolved. Add the rind and lemon juice. Beat in the cheese, together with the sifted flour.

Whip the egg-whites until they stand in peaks and fold them into the cheese mixture. Pour the mixture into the baked flan case, sprinkle evenly with the flaked almonds and bake at Gas 3, Electricity 325° for 40 to 45 minutes.

Turn off the heat but leave the cheese cake to cool in the oven for 20 minutes. Remove the flan ring during this last 20 minutes. When cold, dredge the top of the cake with icing sugar.

# The Queen's Custard
# or Alexandra Cream

I suppose Miss Acton had Queen Charlotte in mind (wife of George III) when she cooked up this receipt.

I made it for 'Himself' (Edward VII), and he asked me to send how I make it to the Palace; the Queen (Alexandra) being Danish like, had a tooth for this sort of thing.

'He' told me their Chef — I never did get to meet him — always served it in their best Waterford custard cups!

*An Eliza Acton recipe* On the beaten and strained yolks of twelve new-laid eggs pour a pint and a half of boiling cream which has been sweetened, with three ounces of sugar; add the smallest pinch of salt, and thicken the custard as usual. When nearly cold, flavour it with a glass and a half of noyau, maraschino, or cuirasseau, and add the sliced almonds or not, at pleasure.

Yolks of eggs, 12; cream, 1½ pints; sugar, 3 ozs.; little salt; noyau, maraschino, or cuirasseau (white, or orange curaçao), 1½ wineglassfuls.

# Isabella Beeton's Syllabub

## Ingredients

10 macaroons
1 pint cream
4 ozs. castor sugar
Juice of one lemon
The finely grated rind
   of half a lemon

1 small wineglassful
   of sherry or
   Madeira
A pinch of ground
   cinnamon, essence
   of ratafia

## Method

Mix the sugar, lemon juice and rind, cinnamon and wine together in a large basin, add a few drops of essence of ratafia, stir until the sugar is dissolved, then add the cream and whip to a froth. Arrange the macaroons compactly on the bottom of a deep dish, and as the froth is formed on the syllabub skim it off and place it on the biscuits. When the whole of the preparation has been reduced to a froth, stand the dish in a cold place, and let it remain for at least 12 hours before serving.

# An Apple Charlotte,
## or Charlotte de Pommes

*An Eliza Acton recipe* Butter a plain mould (a round or square cake tin will answer the purpose quite well), and line it entirely with thin slices of the crumb of a stale loaf (i.e. slices of bread with the crusts removed), cut so as to fit into it with great exactness, and dipped into clarified butter. When this is done, fill the mould to the brim with apple marmalade; cover the top with slices of bread dipped in butter, and on these place a dish, a large plate, or the cover of a French stewpan with a weight upon it. Send the Charlotte to a brisk oven for three-quarters of an hour should it be small, and for an hour if large. Turn it out with great care, and serve it hot. If baked in a slack oven it will not take a proper degree of colour, and it will be liable to break in the dishing. The strips of bread must of course join very perfectly, for if any spaces were left between them the syrup of the fruit would escape and destroy the good appearance of the dish: should there not have been sufficient marmalade prepared to fill the mould entirely, a jar of quince or apricot jam, or of preserved cherries even, may be added to it with advantage. The butter should be well drained from the Charlotte before it is taken from the mould; and sugar may be sifted thickly over it before it is served, or it may be covered with any kind of clear red jelly.

A more elegant, and we think an easier mode of forming the crust, is to line the mould with small rounds of bread stamped out with a plain cake or paste cutter, then dipped in butter, and placed with the edges sufficiently one over the other to hold the fruit securely: the strips of bread are sometimes arranged in the same way.

Make this up proper and with careful attention like what Miss Acton tells you and you'll have the best pudding ever.

I've got my girls to do like she says at the end; cut out all them circles; worth all the bother, I can tell you.

# Marmalade for the Charlotte

Weigh 3 lbs. of good boiling apples, after they have been pared, cored, and quartered; put them into a stewpan with 6 ounces of fresh butter, three-quarters of a pound of sugar beaten to powder, three-quarters of a teaspoonful of pounded cinnamon, and the strained juice of a lemon. Let these stew over a gentle fire, until they form a perfectly smooth and dry marmalade; keep them often stirred that they may not burn, and let them cool before they are put into the crust. This quantity is for a moderate-sized Charlotte.

(*Note* Make your 'Marmalade' with Cox's pippins — it is stunning.)

# Claret Jelly

## Ingredients

1 packet blackcurrant-
   flavoured jelly
1 pint claret or
   claret-type wine

Zest of 1 orange
1 oz. castor sugar
Unsweetened whipped
   cream for decoration

## Method

Take the zest of the orange with a potato peeler — this eliminates getting much of the bitter white pith on the flavoursome orange peel. Finely shred this zest and place in a basin, together with the sugar and jelly cubes.

Bring the claret to just under boiling point and pour it into the basin, stirring until all the jelly is dissolved. Allow to cool, then pour into a wetted mould and put to set.

Decorate with lots of unsweetened whipped cream.

# Rich Suet Crust

## Ingredients

8 ozs. flour
3 ozs. fresh dry white
   breadcrumbs
3 ozs. suet

3 ozs. butter
1 heaped teaspoon baking
   powder
Approx. $\frac{1}{3}$ pint water
Pinch of salt

## Method

Have the butter hard; grate this on a coarse grater; sieve flour, salt and baking powder together. Mix grated butter, flour etc. together. Mix quickly to a soft dough with water. Do not knead.

Roll out lightly and deftly on a well-floured board.

*Note* We brought a deal of interest into our suet crusts at the Bentinck by adding a bit of grated lemon or orange rind for sweet puddings; cinnamon if it was for a rhubarb pudding.

Mace, nutmeg, bay, sage can all be introduced for savoury meat puddings.

# Choux Pastry

## Ingredients

3 ozs. butter
$3\frac{3}{4}$ ozs. plain white flour

3 eggs
$1\frac{1}{2}$ gills water

## Method

For choux pastry the flour must be dry and sieved through a

fine meshed sieve. Bring the butter and water to the boil; remove from the heat. Add the flour to the liquid at one fell swoop. Using a flat sided spatula, beat until smooth and the mixture definitely leaves the sides of the pan.

Leave to cool but not to get quite cold. Beat the eggs lightly, and then *gradually* beat into the paste; continue beating at this stage until shiny.

Fill into a piping bag. Lightly butter a baking tray. Pipe out the desired shapes and bake. Don't take the buns out until quite dry and firm.

*Note* Start with a cool oven and raise the temperature to 425° (Gas 7) as soon as the choux buns are put in.

# Ice-Creams

Whilst we all know that ice-creams are as old as the Chinese, it took President Madison to popularise them in the Western world back in 1815 when they had a little to-do in the kitchens at the old White House.

The cooks had put their custards and creams into the iceboxes and forgotten them; they came out cold and solid and that started them thinking. Having served them in this state with great success they delved into their books and came up with all sorts of old recipes for ice-creams and what have you; they've been popular ever since.

We always make our own ice-cream at the Bentinck: this way we can have them as rich as we like, and can have what flavours and blends we like as well.

The ladies are very fond of iced puddings when they are brought to dine with us, and if I know the lady in question — and I usually do — then I might make a special one in a special shape and colour (like I intended for Belinda Travers, didn't I?) to fit in with her particular personal taste in clothes; or if she's a lady from the theatre or music hall, I'll try to find a shape that will fit the theme: a heart for a love story; a shoe for a ballet dancer (Belinda Travers got a *swan* because she was a ballet dancer, and you don't get a prize for guessing which bleedin' ballet!)

Before I give you my recipes, let me explain just what all the Frenchified terms about ice-creams mean.

The differences between one and the other are not very much, so there's no need to get into a sweat about it. Generally speaking, a plain water ice is a *granita*. Like its Italian name tells you, it's slightly grainy because you don't stir it at all, but just put it to set.

For a *sorbet*, a beaten egg white is added in different proportions depending whether you like it harder or softer.

A *sherbet* is an extra soft sorbet.

A *Bombe* — and this is what it's all about in the hotel and restaurant business — is a fancy mould lined with different sorts, colours and flavours of ice-cream, the centre often packed with macerated fruits, nuts, crushed macaroons, candied fruits and suchlike. It is a good piece of theatre for the likes of Mrs Wellkin and Mrs Cochrane and the girls to let rip with their imagination, for there are no hard or fast rules about what goes with what. *Bombes, Parfaits* and Iced Mousses all come under the general heading of iced puddings at the Bentinck.

If you are making ice-cream at home, you might well not have one of these machines like we professionals have, so you'll have to use crushed ice and saltpetre and improvise with a smaller drum (the churn) fitted into a larger drum which will contain the ice and salt mixture. You'll need quite a bit of patience as you'll have to stir the thing by hand, using a spatula to keep the sides — where it freezes first — clear.

The freezing mixture consists of sodium chloride (sea salt or freezing salt) and saltpetre. The action of the two salts upon the ice causes a marked drop in temperature which readily congeals any contiguous liquids (i.e. the basic custard or sorbet mixture).

Care must be taken that the salt doesn't get into the custard mixture, so only pack the ice to two-thirds the way up the sides of the middle drum or 'churn'.

Use a ratio of 1½ lbs. salt and 4 ozs. saltpetre to 10 lbs. of crushed ice.

*Note* Today we would use a deep freeze, but for moulding bombes it is still easier in the first stages to work with the mould set on a container of 'freezing' mixture, again taking scrupulous care that the salt doesn't contaminate the ice-cream. It is also an excellent way of working with aspic.

When making and serving any type of ice-cream, always chill the bowls, whisks and serving dishes.

## Basic Vanilla Ice-Cream

### Ingredients

4 egg-yolks  
A piece of vanilla pod  

3 ozs. castor sugar  
½ pint double cream

### Method

Cream the yolks and sugar until almost white and all the sugar particles are dissolved. Bring the cream to the boil with the vanilla pod in. Pour onto the creamed yolks, stirring very well all the time. Over the gentlest of heats (if you are nervous, arrange the bowl over a pan of simmering water, but ensure the bottom is in contact with the water) thicken the 'custard' but do not let it boil: it should well-coat the back of a *wooden* spoon, about as thick as 'double' cream.

Leave to cool completely. Remove the vanilla pod. Pour the mixture into an ice-cream maker (following the instructions given with your particular machine) or into the ice trays of your refrigerator — or use plastic boxes, tested for size to ensure they fit into the ice-making compartment.

When the cream is half-frozen, after about half-an-hour (but you'll need to watch this for yourself), tip the contents into a chilled bowl and give it a whip up before returning it to the trays for final freezing. This helps prevent ice granules forming.

# Basic Sugar Syrup for Ices

## Ingredients

8 ozs. white sugar                    1 pint water
Juice of half a lemon

## Method

Dissolve the sugar in the water and bring it to the boil. Let it boil at a gentle roll for 10 minutes — (if you are using a universal thermometer, it should get to 240°F. 110°C; or soft ball).

Remove the pan from the heat; take off any scum (some sugars are quite dirty),strain through a muslin and add the lemon juice. Let it cool completely.

For fruit ices, mix half-a-pint of basic syrup with half-a-pint of fruit purée or juice.

# Pineapple Ice

This is nice when served in a half pineapple shell, which should be well chilled. Spikes of angelica can be stuck into whipped cream blobs, to simulate pineapple foliage.

Grate 1 pint of fresh pineapple. Mix with 1 pint of basic syrup; rub the whole through a fine sieve (use a blender). Add the juice of half a lemon, plus a tablespoon of Kirsch. (If you have problems freezing this, you may have to resort to using a sugar measure (saccharometer) and it should read 20°.)

# Lemon Ice

Zest 3 lemons and leave this to soak in the basic syrup. Add the strained juice of 3 lemons and 2 oranges. Follow the recipe for freezing water ices, adding a whisked egg-white if you want a softer finish.

# Tangerine Ice

Zest 4 tangerines and infuse the zest in the basic stock syrup. Then add the strained juice of 6 tangerines, 1 lemon and 2 oranges before freezing as in the other recipes.

# Chocolate Ice-Cream

Dissolve 4 ozs. bitter chocolate in the cream as you heat it for the basic vanilla ice-cream recipe (p. 197).

# Walnut Ice-Cream

Infuse 3 ozs. of crushed walnuts in the cream, and proceed as for basic vanilla ice-cream. Do not strain the nuts out.

# Coffee Ice-Cream

One (or more) ounces high roast coffee beans: well-crushed, heated gently in the bottom of the pan before the cream is added, and brought to the boil. Proceed as in basic vanilla ice-cream; this recipe need not be strained.

Here are one or two of the *Bombes* we serve at the Bentinck.

# Bombe Duke Street

Line a mould with a half-inch layer of rum-flavoured cream ice; fill the centre with apricot ice mixed with chopped crystallised apricots.

# Bombe Louisa Trotter

Make three linings, half-inch thick, of chocolate, vanilla and coffee ice-creams, leaving the centre of the *bombe* large enough to take a goodly portion of black cherries macerated in rum. These must be well drained and well packed.

# Bombe Clara Schumann

Line the mould with praline ice-cream, add a second lining of orange ice-cream and fill the centre with caramel oranges mixed with brittle praline.

'Charlie's room at the Bentinck, the setting for our "love" dinner . . .'

# Bombe 'Lac Des Cygnes' Louise

I remember when I made my first ice-cream swan — which was to become a right speciality at the Bentinck — (I had a little copper swan mould in my collection at the hotel, and this is what prompted me.)

Charlie Haslemere — well, he was still Charlie Tyrell then — had asked one of his lady friends, Belinda Travers — Mrs Basil Travers no less — to dine with him.

She wasn't to know what Charlie had in mind: I did, mind you! Special flowers, my Quail Pudding, and *no garlic,* he says. Well, she stood him up good and proper when she found out his little game! Poor Charlie, he was taken aback, but he turned the tables on me, and not half! He was a right Casanova — 'Louisa,' he says, 'will you do me the honour of dining with me . . .'

Well, what with all that Clicquot Rosé and Montrachet and Claret . . . ! I'd planned a real delight for him and his lady, my baby swan made from vanilla ice-cream, all snuggled up in a bed of little meringues filled with liqueur cream with brandy cherries blazing away in silver boats, and angelica and glittering silver balls.

Well, it was to be a romantic evening, wasn't it!

But we all know what happened to me. I fell good and proper, didn't I? But I've not regretted a minute of it. You don't have to have an actual swan — well, the same might happen to you mightn't it — if you're lucky: a couple of scallop shells sandwiched together makes a pretty substitute, or just any nice shape prettied up — making it pretty's what it's all about.

Here's how to set about it then.

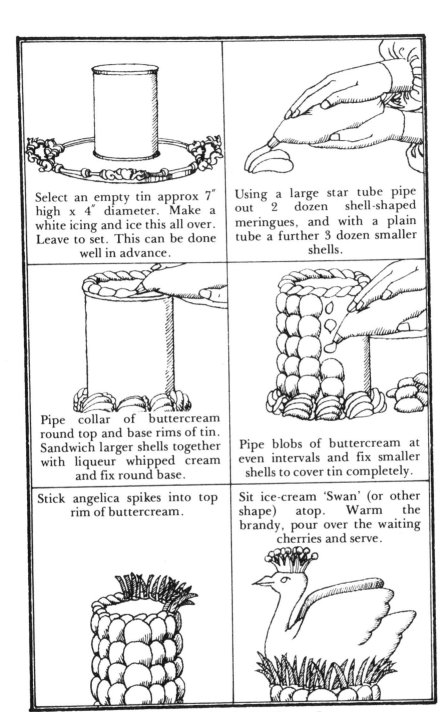

Select an empty tin approx 7″ high x 4″ diameter. Make a white icing and ice this all over. Leave to set. This can be done well in advance.

Using a large star tube pipe out 2 dozen shell-shaped meringues, and with a plain tube a further 3 dozen smaller shells.

Pipe collar of buttercream round top and base rims of tin. Sandwich larger shells together with liqueur whipped cream and fix round base.

Pipe blobs of buttercream at even intervals and fix smaller shells to cover tin completely.

Stick angelica spikes into top rim of buttercream.

Sit ice-cream 'Swan' (or other shape) atop. Warm the brandy, pour over the waiting cherries and serve.

How to assemble the Ice-Cream Swan

203

The finished Swan.

204

# Vanilla Ice-Cream

This is a very rich ice-cream; for a somewhat plainer, but equally delicious form, substitute milk for cream.

## Ingredients

1 pint single cream
Vanilla pod

8 egg-yolks
3 ozs. castor sugar

## Method

Beat the egg-yolks and sugar until they are creamy and thick and all the sugar has dissolved. Bring the cream to the boil, together with the vanilla pod. Remove the pod and pour the cream onto the eggs and sugar, whisking well all the time.

Arrange this bowl over a pan of boiling water and, stirring all the time, thicken the 'custard' until it well-coats the back of a *wooden* spoon.

Leave the custard to cool completely, then chill; either follow the instructions for your particular machine, or place in a suitable container in the ice-making compartment of your refrigerator (or in the deep freeze).

# Liqueur Cream

## Ingredients

½ pint thick cream          NO sugar
Tablespoon Orange Curaçao

## Method

Blend the two ingredients together, and whip until of a piping consistency.

# Liqueur Butter Cream

## Ingredients

6 ozs. unsalted butter
8 ozs. icing sugar

2 tablespoons Orange
    Curaçao
1 egg-yolk

## Method

Beat butter until soft and light. Beat in yolk; add liqueur, beating well in. Gradually incorporate the icing sugar.

# Wines

I can't deny that my cellar improved after Old Side-Whiskers (Major Smith-Barton) dumped himself on us at the Bentinck. I say 'dumped', because it wasn't never his intention to cause us bother, but if you will get yourself and your money mixed up with the gee-gees then some day you're going to be out of luck and come a right cropper; and that's just what happened to him.

I couldn't help feeling sorry for the old lad, well he wasn't that old, he'd done a good stint in the army so he might 'ave been pushing fifty. So, when he couldn't meet his bills I agreed he should earn his keep; helping Starr in the front hall, portering and polishing a bit, and giving me a bit of a hand with the cellar stock books.

I'd always liked, and only drunk, Champagne. The good ones, mind you, none of your big loose-bubbled stuff, but the fine foamy Champagnes like Dom Pérignon, Krug, Mumm. But in the hotel business you have to get to know, and like, a lot more than the best and the Major was to learn me.

'Old Weary-Britches, Merriman, decanting.'

It wasn't long before he'd taken control of the lot and, gentleman that he was, gently showed me a thing or two about wines and how to keep them and serve them. Mind you, he *should* know a lot; came from a good family where they'd always had a good cellar; he even told me that on his mother's side — the Bartons — that they had French connections at Château Léoville-Barton, it could be right. And I wouldn't mind guessing he'd had a pipe or two of port put down for him when he was born. Then followed Eton and one of the big Universities — finished him off as they say — and we all know what fine cellars these colleges still have.

Member of Boodles he was for a time, and his father before him, and his grandfather, so that's a bit of vintage family stuff before we start.

I didn't even bother to write down what he showed me until now; but I didn't forget anything neither.

He was a great friend of the Todds, the well-known wine merchants, in his regiment he was together with one of them — I forget which he said it was. I don't want to get grand and high-flown like what a lot of wine bibbers do, because wine's for drinking and nothing else, but there are a few points which will help you to drink better, you might say.

So I've set it down for you to read. All of what I learnt from Old Side-Whiskers was good basic knowledge and ideal for learners. If you master these basics, like I did, you're not going to go far wrong when drinking and serving. And after you've mastered this lot, you might like to buy a few books to read on the matter, because I'm not saying there *aren't* lengths to go to: just that beginners shouldn't feel shy at starting, having a go, but in the right way; so buy it; store it well; look at it; smell it; and drink it up. But remember, what's worth drinking's worth thinking about.

# What is Wine

For my purpose here, wine is the fermented juice of the grape; nothing more. We're not delving into the stillroom mysteries of elderberry, rhubarb and ginger — just black or white grapes, with or without their skins!

The way wine's made is very simple: the grapes are collected and the juice pressed out by treading, and more recently by new developing mechanical contrivances. This juice or 'must' ferments, and then things start to get more complicated. The fermentation is easy to understand: it means the grape juice is converted into alcohol. The sugar causes the fermentation to start. The *chemistry* of fermentation — the inter-action of the yeasts — is the complicated bit, and I'm not going into that part except to tell you that the Major puts it like this:

> The bacteriological process in which living micro-organisms increase and multiply, need the active co-operation of oxygen from the air.
>
> The young wine is then run off into vats or casks and stopped up from the air for the second fermentation to take place in the cask. The wine at this stage becomes quite turbulent, throwing off a deposit which then leaves it clearish. Then the wine is run off into clean sulphured casks, but in order to get it really clear, it is 'fined'; the finings (often egg-whites or gelatine) carry any remaining suspended particles to the bottom of the cask.

Get this in your noddle and you'll understand the whole thing; it's not much to learn for a beginner. Mind you, there are variations on these essential processes. Next comes the wait before getting it into bottles.

Good wines will be left in casks from 2 to 4 years before bottling, corking and labelling.

Smith-Barton's next little lesson — we always sat in my office late at night with a good bottle of port or Madeira between us while I listened to him moaning on; he was a dull old stick at times, but get him on the gee-gees and the wines and he livened up enough to keep me quiet, and listening — was when he told me the differences between 'natural', 'made' and 'fortified' wines. 'Natural' wines being the still wines of France, Germany and Italy (and those other grubby little countries we won't mention here). They depend for their varied character on the type of vine, the quality of the soil, position, aspect of the vineyard, climate, and the eventual state of the weather at vintage time. It's all simple and logical like I like things isn't it? Remember all that lot, and then remember that they are made and matured like the Major tells us earlier, and you'll have got your basics straight in five minutes!

My favourite, Champagne, is a 'made' wine; all sparkling wines are made by trapping the fermentation inside the bottle. This makes it bubble and that's why the bottles need that wire contraption on the cork — to hold it in.

I've always been told it was a God-following monk who discovered this by accident when he was playing with the bottles at the monastry instead of gettin' down on 'is knees. *He* had a patron saint or guardian-angel, didn't he? And it doesn't take a genius to guess his name — Dom Pérignon. Only those wines what are made in the Champagne district of France near Ay and Épernay should be called 'Champagne'. The French are going to have a right battle on their hands one day, because everybody's making sparkling wine and calling it 'champagne'. But you stick to the quality names and you'll be all right.

Port and sherry are 'fortified' wines. This means 'strengthened' and Old Side-Whiskers says this is done by adding *wine-spirit* — brandy — to the wine, which checks the normal process where the sugar in the grape juice is converted into alcohol. This leaves the wine characteristically sweet to a greater or lesser degree, just how much is added is left up to the individual maker.

To colour these wines when they aren't perhaps deep enough, red wine is boiled down 'til it is dark and thick, and a little added where necessary.

The Major says they get up to all sort of tricks at the cheap end of the trade. But we're not interested in rubbish at the Bentinck, so we'll not concern ourselves with it here neither.

Port comes, or should only come, from the Douro district of Portugal. Sherry from Xères or Jerez in Spain.

The Major is forever telling me that the general terms Claret, Burgundy, Sherry etc. are too general to denote specific quality. The cleverness of wine lies in the particular grape used. The best names in wines are made from distinct varieties of grapes. So after getting this little lot straight we end up with the weather; this finally decides the specific quality of the particular vintage and also creates great interest for the men in their clubs as they sniff and swirl and peer and ponder. There's only one real exception to this and that's in California where the weather behaves itself: not that I've been there yet, but I've tried their wines in New York at Wally's (Waldorf Astor) Hotel on Park Avenue. Good they was too.

*Tasting* Wine is savoured both by sense of taste and sense of smell; there are those what'll argue on the philosophy of these two senses being different, but they are to me. Mind you, I've known people who, when blindfolded, can't tell port from sherry. There are also those what claim and state that acids, salts, albumen, ether and such like make for taste and bouquet. Well, I'm all for leaving those clever folk where they are: necessary they may be (as Chemists) dull they are without doubt!

*Glass* Albeit the Almighty gave you a decent nose and palate, the next thing you'll need — apart from some wine — is a decent glass. I know at the Bentinck we have a whole forest of glasses. But I also know what makes a table look nice — and glasses do. So that's why we have 'em, and also because most folk are snobbish and like to think they know which glass is for what. We can all learn that if we have to; I mean white wine glasses an ounce or two smaller than red wine ones; longer stems for Hocks and Moselles and so on.

I'm waiting for the day when we get down to just one or two basic shapes; so I'll give you my ideas here and now. Call them Mrs Trotter's types, if you like; but I know you'll agree there's some good commonsense in what I say.

For your table wines the glass has to be big enough to hold enough without wetting the carpet and staining the tablecloth

3 perfect glass shapes l to r: All purpose white or red wine glass; Sherry, Port, Madeira glass; Champagne and sparkling wine.

when you swirl it round; why swirl it round? Commonsense. Just like Old Side-Whiskers learnt me; to coat the sides of the glass with wine which will help you get more of the lovely bouquet. So pick a glass big enough (8 fluid ozs.). Then a stem long enough to get your fingers round without contacting the bowl of the glass. Keep white wines cool, like they should be, and if you need to chivvy your red wine up a bit, just cup the glass in both hands and that'll do it nice and gentle. I always remember Gus (my ex — Augustus Trotter) showing me this when we was tasting that Château d'Yquem he was serving when H.M. (Edward VII) first came to Lord Henry Norton's place in Curzon Street. Now I come to think of it, he (Gus) also learnt me a lot about wine. What was it he said once about a Trittenheimer —

'. . . I think we could risk something a little lighter, Miss Leyton . . . a Chablis perhaps . . . something drier . . . or something fresh, gay and charming from the Moselle, a Trittenheimer Falkenberg . . .'

Then this big glass we've got; with a nice 4 inch stem, should just curve in a bit at the top; stops the spills and holds the bouquet like what I've just said. For my favourite tipple, Champagne, there's all sorts about. Saucers, saucers with square sides, flutes, flutes with hollow stems, but I think somebody should make a glass a bit like a tulip. Until they do we'll have to manage with the flutes, but not never those b . . . y saucers. All up your arms it goes *and* all over the carpet; and as for swizzle sticks, daft idea I think to want to get rid of the bubbles when somebody's gone to all the bother to put them in!

For brandy, those *little* balloons is all right and I use these also for liqueurs — just you try it, fair makes your head reel when you sniff deep.

For my sherry I think a nice shaped 4 ounce glass will do (a Spanish copeta type is popular today) and the same for port; but with a nice stem. And if you want to show off with cut glass then I suppose here's where you'll do it with your port glass.

*How to taste* When the Major first showed me how to taste, we had a right carry on, I can tell you. Well, I didn't believe him at first when he said:

'Mrs Trotter, take the type of glass I describe, then pour a *little* wine into it. Hold the glass by the stem and swirl it round to coat the sides, which operation will release the maximum bouquet from your wine — (he was right, it did). Now draw a little wine into your mouth and hold it there. Now comes the difficult part: draw air through your teeth *and* the wine, and you will find that this releases even more of the wine's flavours. Swirl it round in your mouth, and spit it out.'

Not at all ladylike, I can tell you, as he spat into my fireplace. But if the thing is to be done, then it might as well be done proper. So for future tasting, I got Old Starr to fill a pail with sawdust. Mind you, I used to make sure the office door was locked when we were at it: didn't want nobody catching me making a fool of myself (or so I thought until I realised that the Major was absolutely right).

It really is the only way to get your tastebuds coated, which are all over your mouth in different places, and it's these tastebuds that tell you all about the wine: how much tannin,

214

sugar, acidity and such like.

Mind you, you won't learn all this in a week. Takes years. But you've got to start somewhere, and the men have been at it for centuries, so I don't see why the ladies what want to learn shouldn't join in.

I might add that I didn't do much gargling and spitting at first; I thought it was too good to waste, until I gradually realised what a lot I was learning about wines. I enjoy a good tasting session nowadays.

*Decanting and serving* Now about decanting. We've always been very particular at the Bentinck.

We decant *all* red wines and even white ones sometimes. Air never did wine worth its metal any harm — except specials (old and rare wines) and you've got to watch they don't breathe too soon or they'll breathe their last before you've caught 'em.

There are a few tools and gadgets any wine butler worth his metal's got to have when decanting, and they're these:

A proper corkscrew with a good wide thread that won't pull the core of the cork away like some narrow gimlet screws do. There was a time — perhaps there still are some — when you could buy a good corkscrew with a hammer and brush handle (see p. 216) useful for opening bottles of vintage port where the tops are wax-sealed.

Some wines have very difficult corks — tight — and the best type of screw for dealing with these is a double-lever 'butterfly' extractor. Watch when you start levering that the cork is on the move and the screw isn't pulling through.

If you have a good stock of vintage port, a pair of port tongs is going to help. Old Merriman is as nervous as Old Nick when he's using these, but the Major showed me how to go about it easy like. You really only need use these if you're in bother with a tricky cork.

The tongs should be heated on the gas or in the fire 'til they're bright red hot. Then grip the bottle's neck under the flange. When the red glow has subsided, remove the tongs to a safe place, then have a wet cloth ready, and wrap this round the neck where the tongs have gripped it. It will 'crack' off easily. (That's why we say 'crack a bottle of port' isn't it?)

Hammer & brush Combined
corkscrew: seal hammer and
brush.

Whenever you are drawing any cork, it is a good idea to
protect your hands with a glass-cloth — or even an old glove.
You never know when there might be a flaw in the glass, and
you don't want a cut hand, do you? So better safe than sorry, I
say.

Now, there's a lot of those wicker wine cradles about for
moving and tilting bottles. I don't hold with these. Nor does
the Major, nor does old weary britches.

No matter how carefully you handle these 'baby's cots',
you're bound to get a bit of 'back-swish', and that's just what
you don't want when serving good wine. My motto is: decant it
once and for all, and enjoy the pleasure of seeing the light play
on the wine in a nice glass decanter on your dinner table.
Remember, the eye plays a very important part in wine
drinking, so start the seduction process early.

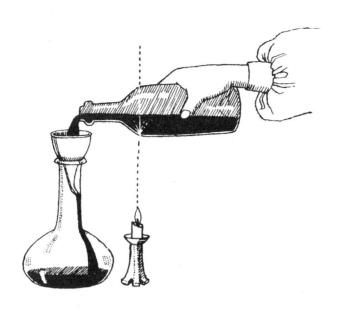

Decanting wine, showing eye-
line over candle.

Those of you who have a smart silver decanting funnel, use it. That's what it's for, not to sit on the shelf in the cabinet. Keep it well washed in hot water. No silver polish! No soap. If you do have to clean it, then boil it afterwards, and dry it. The turned end of the funnel directs the wine down the inside of the decanter and prevents it frothing.

Generally speaking when serving wine it's white before red; dry before sweet; young before old when serving two reds together. If things are more complicated than this, then you'll have to have a word with the experts; and there's plenty of them around ready to bore you out of your tiny mind — one thing to remember, which I've found out for myself; never serve a sweet dessert wine with the food. Always pour it just before; give the wine a chance to show its worth, without battling against the cook's possible heavy hand with the sugar.

217

3 decanter shapes from l to r: Sherry decanter, Spirit decanter, Claret jug.

In summer, Champagne and white wines should be served 'from the ice'. In winter, except for Champagne, they might well be cool enough from your cellar. Don't never put ice into your wine; ice melts and weakens it. If you want to cool a wine-cup or cider-punch just fill a pint glass with chipped ice and stand this in your punch bowl. Wines drunk too cold lose a lot of their flavour and interest.

Here's some illustrations of nice decanter shapes and a claret jug and position of the hands while decanting. As you know, at the Bentinck, we serve like in a country house, so there's no need to wrap up all your bottles like a doll in a cot. Those bottles that have been on ice need a wipe, so you just need a clean linen napkin in your left hand to dab away any drips when you pour into a glass. Never fill a glass more than a third to half full; red, white or pink. You've got to have room for the delicious bouquet we've been talking about, to develop. Here's a few temperatures for you to remember:

Cellar temperature, 53° to 58°, and constant at that. Don't *store* wine near a boiler or fireplace. Red wines are served at room temperature, 65° to 70°, and should be up-ended *in the cellar* and brought carefully out of your cellar at least six to eight hours before decanting. White wines are best served cooled (not 'iced') at 55°. Young Beaujolais is often served cooled and some Italian red wines are nicer for cooling.

There's a lot of old rubbish talked about wines and a lot of adjectives used that make me blush they're that fancy. But if you want to communicate what's in your mind (and in your glass) then some words on the subject will be needed.

Old Side-Whiskers and I have gone through a lot of the more usual and necessary terminology and come up with the following list for you to learn and use next time you're bibbing.

# A glossary of terms

*Age, Ageing* The characteristics of age in time are: first, progressive softening up to a point (mainly due to deposition of tartar, hence tartar is so often found on the insides of casks); and, secondly, the development of bouquet of a secondary nature (due, it is said, to the action of micro-organisms).

*Beverage Wines or Table Wines* Opposed to vintage wines. Wines of average quality and strength (and price) suitable for drinking in large quantities and regularly.

*Body* That quality in a wine which gives it the appearance of consistency and vinous strength. Merchants speak of a 'full' wine or wine with 'body', as opposed to a light, cold, or thin wine.

*Bond* Wine or spirits, etc., are kept 'in bond' in State-controlled warehouses till the duty is paid on them.

*Bouquet* The odour or perfume of fine wine.

*Brut* Of Champagne, with no added sugar or liqueur. 'Nature' means the same.

*Château-Bottled* In Bordeaux. Quality vintage wines bottled at the Château where grown, instead of by the wine merchant. Similarly, 'estate-bottled' in Burgundy and Germany.

*Cordial* A lighter kind of liqueur made by infusion of alcohol and sugar with fruit juices.

*'Corked'* Wine that is corked tastes mouldy; it also smells bad. Corked wine is rare, and wine-drinkers in a restaurant should be careful before they make the accusation. No restaurateur would refuse to replace a corked bottle or would make a mistake about the condition. A few particles of cork-dust falling into the wine do not constitute 'corked' wine — as has been occasionally thought by ignorants. Sometimes the corks of the bottles are too porous or of inferior quality and give the wine a bad taste, this taste the French term, 'goût de bouchon'.

*Crû* Growth. A particular quality growth is described as 'a premier crû', 'grand crû', etc.

*Crust* A deposit in old wines, especially Port, Burgundies, and red wines generally.

*Cuvée* Contents of a cellar; also the different products of pressure of one vine which fill many vats; more particularly applied to Champagne, but sometimes to Burgundy.

*Dry* Opposed to sweet — with no excess of sugar.

*Fine Champagne* 'Grande' or 'Fine' Champagne is the official description given to finest quality *Brandies* from the Grande or Fine Champagne district. (Not to be confused with wines of the Champagne district).

*Fiery* Applied to raw spirits or raw wine; meaning is obvious.

*Fining* The process of clarification of a wine by introduction of albumen, e.g. white of egg or other suitable medium.

*Fliers* Light, whitish particles that float in white wines or rest at the bottom, looking like a light sand. An effect apparently of transportation to colder countries than the country of origin. They do not affect the taste of the wine. A cure is to rest the bottles in a warm temperature, say about 70°F.

*Fortifying* By the addition of wine-spirit, e.g. to Port and Sherry in the making.

*Frappé* Of sparkling wine, iced sufficiently for the table (and liqueurs served over crushed ice).

*Green* Of young, immature wine.

*Must* The grape juice before it becomes wine by fermentation.

*Nature* Same as 'Brut'.

*Phylloxera* Phylloxera vastatrix: an insect pest destroying the vine. Appeared in France 1865, and was at its worst 1868-1873.

*Pipe* Cask for Port and Tarragona wines, 56 dozen bottles or 115 gallons.

*Proof* A standard estimate alcoholic strength of a spirit.

*Racking* Separating the bright wine from the deposit.

*Ruby* Term to describe a Port midway between Tawny and Full — of a reddish tinge.

*Solera* Of Sherry: double butts of stock wines used for maintaining the standard of shipped Sherries.

*Tawny* Refers to colour and character of Port; of wines that have matured in wood (contrast with Ruby and Vintage).

*Ullage* An ullaged cask or bottle is one, some of the contents of which have leaked, evaporated, or been extracted.

*Vin Ordinaire* Used of wines of lesser quality in comparison with the finer wines of same district.

*Vintage Wines* Of wines of high character. Used principally of Ports, Clarets, Burgundies, and Sauternes; shipped under their respective years.

*Woody* A wine may become tainted from a defective or rotten stave in the cask. If discovered early enough the wine may be saved by racking off into a clean, well-sulphured cask.

*'Worn' (or 'tired')* Of Brandy: from being too long in cask. Also of Clarets, etc., that have been left too long in bottle.

# Wines and When to serve them

| French | Spanish | Italian | Portu-guese | Dish |
|---|---|---|---|---|
| Vermouth | Dry Pale Sherry | Vermouth | | Hors d'Oeuvre Fish and Soup |
| Graves* Chablis* | | | | Oysters and other Shell Fish Fish Pasta |
| | Sherry* | Marsala* | Madeira* | Soup |
| Sauternes* Chablis* Alsace* Most other white Burgundies | | | | Foie Gras Smoked Fish (Salmon, Mackerel, Trout etc) Fish Fruit and *before* Sweets |

| | | | | |
|---|---|---|---|---|
| Claret** | Chianti** | | Most Roasts (Meat, Poultry, Game) and Cheese Dishes | |
| Fine Claret** Fine Burgundy** | Chianti** | | Most Roasts | |
| Champagne* | | | Anytime | |
| | | Madeira* | Pastry, Sweets Cheese | |
| | Malaga** | Port** | Cheese Fruit, Nuts, Fruit Cakes | |
| Brandy** Liqueurs* | | | Coffee (after) | |

\* Serve at cool temp. or 'off the ice' in Summer
\*\*Serve at temperature of room

'Old Side-Whiskers, Major Smith-Barton.'

# Louisa Trotter
# on Smoking

Real ladies don't smoke, not even in my hotel: NOT NEVER. And gentlemen don't smoke before dinner, and when they do smoke the ladies leave them to it, and go to the drawing-room.

In private houses of any standing there'll be a room set apart for smoking and the gentlemen will wear smoking jackets so they don't get all their other clothes all smelly.

Mind you — and I must confess this always bothered me — it was Himself (Edward VII) what started the fashion for long cigars, but of course I couldn't say anything about that unsociable little habit, could I?

He was also a whisky-and-soda man like a lot of young cavalry officers were. The 1914-18 war helped to sort them out when they were introduced to the (officers) mess port. They didn't serve vintage stuff to these youngsters, who were too wet behind the ears to know what was what in a port decanter — some of them were only eighteen when they were commissioned, so how could they — but it did introduce them to the port drinking habit and all that stuff about passing it clockwise.

And they all knew they couldn't light up until they'd drunk a loyal toast to H.M. the King, so that checked their smoking habits a bit.

I understand that there are certain ladies — women — I call them *demi-mondaines* — who are pushing to make smoking fashionable. Lady Warwick's one of them, and she was a member of the Marlborough House set. I heard she'd introduced long ivory cigarette holders from Paris, but it will be a long time before that catches on here if I can help it, and like I said, not never in my hotel.

I seem to remember Miss Irene Baker used to have a puff on the quiet and she met her come-uppance, and not half!

# Christmas at
# the Bentinck

The nicest time of the year for most folk is Christmas time, not that I'm what you might call a real God-following churchgoer, but I do like to slip into St James's Church in Piccadilly every now and then and sort things out, as you might say: just me and Him, so to speak. That's why each Christmas Eve the vicar from St James's sends the choir over to sing carols, we all being still good friends. The little lads look lovely in their red cassocks and starched white ruffs, holding their lanterns up by their sides, so they can see what they're singing about, and we all join in — Starr, Mary and Mrs Cochrane, the lot. Even old Merriman has a grunt or two. The guests all gather at the bottom of the stairs, and Fred has a sprig of holly in his collar, and a glass or two of my special punch makes sure they all enter into the spirit of the occasion.

I've had most of me staff since I bought the Bentinck and they look forward to our sort of Christmas Eve just like kids going to a party; usually Johnny — that's Major Farjeon — sends us a huge tree and Charlie always makes sure plenty of holly and mistletoe comes down from his Yorkshire estate. What with this and plenty of spruce and fir branches about the place, the hotel pillars twined round with silver tinsel, festive with red bows and baubles dripping from everything, we soon have it all looking fit for the Three Kings to march into.

Starr really goes to town in the courtyard, hanging Chinese lanterns in all the plants and shrubs and looping them round the window tops. Mind you, it's usually too frosty to set foot outside, and anyway who wants to when we've piled the fires high with fir cones. There's nothing like the smell of pine burning to get your nose twitching and your elbow lifting that warm punch. Real Christmassy, it all is.

The men folk muck in and help serve the meal — a right social leveller that little Bentinck habit — come midnight, one of the guests will slip out the back door and come back in through the Duke Street entrance dressed up as Santa Claus to let Christmas in as it should be. Then it's a case of who's in the best voice for 'Christians Awake'. The St James's lads don't get a chance when we all begin, I can tell you. *We've* all had my punch to help us let go, haven't we?

Christmas Day is the only time we ever have everybody together sitting down — meals being usually served in the private dining-rooms. Hired tables are set up in the front hall and in my parlour, and little gilt chairs are sent in from Harrods, with red velvet pads tied to their seats.

I usually like to see to me own flowers, but come Christmas there's too much to do for one, so I get a floral artist in to help me and Mary get things right. Christmas roses, holly berries, poinsettias and evergreens are all wired into huge hoops and linked from the candelabra down the middle of all the tables. Wax tapers burn in all the sticks and sconces, and then we are ready for the real treat . . . a good old traditional Christmas dinner as only we know how to do it in England.

I've usually slipped home to Wanstead in the afternoon with the presents for Mum and Dad, before getting back to my stoves making sure, as usual, that everything is how I'd want it. Then we're off: *foie gras de Strasbourg* all done up in its fancy pots; real turtle soup well-laced with a drop of the hard stuff; a lovely fish course, then a saddle of mutton followed by a

Champagne sorbet before going on to a rich apple-stuffed Yorkshire goose, celery salad and my special Christmas pudding with hard sauce, and, just to keep them happy, cheese fritters and then plenty of luxury fruits to dip into: dates, figs, Carlsbad plums, hot-house pineapples, tangerines and suchlike. Plenty of Champagne, claret and port keeps them all cheerful. They don't want for much when I'm around as you know. And, if they've not had enough, there's always a cold table groaning with hams and pheasants, grouse creams, stuffed turkey, poultry, galantines of veal, pressed tongues and my special Marbl'd Veal (and mine's a sight better than Agnes Marshall's that's for sure, she mightn't like me saying this, but it's true); with apricot moulds, bananas in jelly, Nesselrode Pudding, mince pies and plenty more to go at for sweets.

I've usually had a couple of Stiltons maturing in our own cellars, so there's not much going to be wrong with them so long as they don't get at it with one of those damned long-handled spoons . . . makes my blood boil when I see fellers — and from some of the posh Clubs to boot — *scooping* into the middle of a good Stilton without so much as a care as to what others will get after they've finished maulin' it about. Treat the cheese proper and it'll treat you proper by lasting a long time. Start pouring port wine into it only when it's nearly used up; makes for a good 'potted cheese' I'll grant you that.

At one time they all got their presents on Boxing Day, but now they all have to search round the hotel for hidden parcels; that's a right carry-on, getting *lost* up those dark corridors — well, that's what they say! But it's all part of what makes the Bentinck better than other places. Life's never boring an' dull when Louisa Trotter's in charge of the crackers. Anyone who's rubbed shoulders with me is guaranteed to be interesting in more ways than one.

Mind you, I've got me morals even at Christmas time. I want everybody happy and having a right knees-up and I'll bleedin' well work to make sure they get a good party going, but you'll never get a good party going without giving things a bit of a push. It boils down to the same formula most times: good setting, good food, good drink and plenty of goodwill, as is right at this time of the year.

'Ethel, Mrs Cochrane, Starr, Violet, Mary and Merriman having a glass of Madeira in the Bentinck's staff room.'

# Elizabeth Raffald's Milk Punch

## Ingredients

4 pints rich full
   cream milk
Rind of 6 lemons
2 eggs

¼ pint cold milk
1 pint Jamaica rum
½ pint brandy
4 ozs. castor sugar

Grated nutmeg

## Method

Pare the lemons carefully, avoiding any white pith. Put brandy, rum, sugar and peel to soak in a closed jar for two days, shaking two or three times to ensure that the sugar dissolves.

On the day you wish to make the punch, beat the two eggs with the cold milk. Bring the rest of the milk to boiling point, together with the rind from the jar. Remove the rind just before whisking in the beaten eggs.

Do not return the pan to the heat. Add the liquid, which should be warmed in another pan. Grate a little nutmeg on to the top. Serve in warmed glasses. This punch should be *warm*, not hot.

# Eliza Acton's Receipt for Oxford Bishop

Make several incisions in the rind of a lemon, stick cloves in this and roast the lemon by a slow fire. Put small but equal quantities of cinnamon, cloves, mace and allspice, with a trace of ginger, into a saucepan (enamel) with a half-pint of water;

let it boil until it is reduced one-half. Boil one bottle of port wine, burn a portion of the spirit out of it by applying a lighted taper to the saucepan; put the roasted lemon and spice into the wine, stir it up well, and let it stand near the fire ten minutes.

Rub a few knobs of sugar on the rind of the lemon (not roasted), pour the wine into it, grate in some nutmeg, sweeten it to taste, and serve it up with the lemon and spice floating in it.

# St James Pick-You-Up

This is no more than a simple, but mightily effective Edwardian seltzer.

Mix half and half dry white wine with seltzer or soda water, all well chilled, and drink away. It refreshes, restores, and it rejuvenates!

# Duke Street Yuletide Warming Cup

## Ingredients

2 sweet oranges
4 ozs. lump sugar
1 pint water

½ pint orange juice
Juice of one lemon
½ pint brandy

## Method

Rub sugar lumps on orange skins until well soaked in orange 'oils'. Squeeze the lemon and add to strained orange juice. Bring sugar and juices to boil in enamel pan. Pour in brandy, and serve immediately.

# Porter Cup

Cut two small lemons into thin slivers, and put them into a bowl, carefully leaving out the pips. Pour over them a teacupful of sherry and a pint of porter (a dark-brown ale). Add the eighth of a nutmeg grated; mix all thoroughly, ice and serve.

# Mince Pies

This is our recipe for mincemeat using actual minced meat; (freshly minced beef is still used in the United States of America.)

## Ingredients

$1\frac{1}{2}$ lbs. lean underdone
   roast beef
2 lbs. beef suet
1 lb. stoned raisins
1 lb. picked sultanas
$1\frac{1}{2}$ lbs. apples

*All the above ingredients
  to be chopped and then
   mixed with*
1 lb. well washed and
  dried currants
$\frac{1}{4}$ oz. mixed powdered spice

$1\frac{1}{2}$ lbs. pears
1 lb. mixed peel
$\frac{3}{4}$ lb. blanched and chopped
   Valencia almonds
The thin peel of 2 oranges
  and 2 lemons

Juice from the lemons
  and oranges
$1\frac{1}{2}$ lbs. demerara sugar
$\frac{1}{2}$ pint brandy
$\frac{1}{2}$ pint sherry
$\frac{1}{2}$ pint port

$\frac{1}{2}$ pint Jamaica rum

## Method

Make some puff paste, roll it out $\frac{1}{4}$ inch thick, and line some little plain or fancy patty pans with it; place a teaspoonful or dessertspoonful, or more, of mincemeat in each, according to its size, wet the edges of the paste and cover the mincemeat over with more paste. Brush over the top with beaten-up whole raw egg, and put them in a quick oven for about 5 minutes, then take them out, dust them over with icing sugar to glaze them, and put them back to bake for 15 to 20 minutes.

Dish up in a pile on a dish-paper or napkin, and serve hot.

# Christmas Buttered Oranges

Like I say, ideas don't always come natural: leastways when you need a new one urgent like. In my book collection, I have a copy of Anne Blencowe's little cookery book what she wrote in 1694 no less! It was in this that I found the idea for making oranges up in this way. They look beautiful when they're finished, and all tarted up with little flowers; they taste even more beautiful; and they all love them. I always get asked for these when I'm out cooking for the nobs.

## Ingredients

2 large juicy oranges
2 ozs. castor sugar
5 egg-yolks
1 teaspoon rose water
4 ozs. unsalted butter
¼ pint double cream

1 large piece of soft
   candied orange
Crystallised rose petals
   and extra whipped cream
   for decorating
6 orange 'shells' (see *Note)*

## Method

First prepare the orange 'shells' (see *Note*).

Grate the rind from the 2 oranges — which should give you one level tablespoon when pressed down. Squeeze the juice from the oranges.

Select a round-bottomed basin that will fit nicely and firmly into the top of a pan of boiling water. Mix together in the basin the orange juice and rind, egg-yolks and sugar. Arrange the basin over the water, making sure that the water is in contact with the bottom of it.

Stir the mixture gently, but continuously, with a balloon whisk, until it is thick as a good custard. Take care to scrape the sides of the basin during this operation, but do not whisk too briskly or you will create a foam which will prevent your seeing when the liquid has thickened. When the orange mixture starts to 'ribbon', remove the basin from the top of the pan and stand it in a large bowl of cold water to cool slightly. Continue stirring and add the rose water.

Remove the basin from the cold water. Cut the butter into 1 inch cubes before you begin, so that it is soft but not melted. Whisk these pieces into the mixture, making sure that each one is incorporated before adding the next. Half-whip the cream and fold it into the mixture. Cut the soft candied orange into tiny pieces, or shred it on a grater. As the buttered orange starts to set, fold this into it so that it stays suspended and doesn't all sink to the bottom.

Fill the orange 'shells'. Decorate the top of the buttered oranges when set, with home-made crystallised rose petals pouring from under the 'lid' of the orange.

A simpler decoration is to use a 'rose' piping tube and pipe a band of whipped cream round the rim of the orange base, letting it be somewhat thicker on one side than the other so that the 'lid' stands at an attractive angle.

These oranges look most attractive when nestling in a folded organza napkin, or mounted into a pyramid.

*Note* To empty oranges for filling with buttered orange. Reverse the orange so that the 'stalk' or 'bud' is at the base. Holding a small pointed cook's knife at a diagonal angle, insert the tip into the orange an inch down from the apex, cut round and remove a 'lid'. Traditional zig-zag cutting can be used.

Take a teaspoon, if possible an old one which has a worn and rather sharp edge, and using the palm of the hand as a protective 'wall', scoop and lever out all the orange flesh until the shell is quite clean. Do likewise with the lid. *Take care not to pierce the skin at any point.* You will be left with a 'stalk' of pith sticking up from the bottom of the shell. Cut this out with a sharp knife or pair of scissors. Clean the edges of the base and lid of any bits of unsightly pith. At this stage fix any decoration to the lid with a cocktail stick. Never use wire where it is likely to come into contact with food. It is quite safe to wire any rosebuds or miniature flowers to the stick before pushing it through the orange peel lid; if you have any gutta-percha, a strip can be wound round any wire for extra protection. At Christmas time it is nice to use baubles, tinsel bows, miniature angels, organza petals, or any other notion that takes your fancy. (The juice and flesh from the emptied oranges can be used as juice for breakfast, making squash or adding to other sauces.)

# Bentinck Special Rum Sauce

There's rum sauce, and there's rum sauce, I tell my girls. Get your wrist bending with the bottle and get plenty of spirit into it! It's only Christmas once a year so 'in for a penny's' what I say.

## Ingredients

| | |
|---|---|
| ⅜ pint Sauternes (or other sweet white wine) | 5 egg-yolks |
| 5 tablespoons Jamaica rum | 2 ozs. castor sugar |
| | Rind of 1 lemon |

## Method

Cream the egg-yolks and sugar until every granule of sugar has dissolved. Remove the rind of the lemon with a potato peeler and with a sharp knife, patiently shred this as fine as hair. Add to the egg-yolks and stir in the wine and rum.

Arrange the basin over a pan of boiling water, making sure the water is in contact with the bottom of the basin. Whisk the sauce slowly but continuously until it is as thick as double cream. Remove from the heat and continue whisking until the heat has diminished somewhat.

Keep the sauce warm over a pan of hot, but not boiling water. This time the water must *not* be in contact with the bottom of the basin.

# Tangerine and Rum Sherbet

## Ingredients

½ pint white wine (Muscatel)
Juice and finely grated rind of 2 tangerines

2½ ozs. castor sugar
6 egg-yolks
3 egg-whites
4 fluid ozs. rum

½ pint double cream

## Method

Mix together wine, sugar, rum, juice, rind and yolks. Arrange basin over boiling water and *stir* (don't whisk) until quite thick. Leave to cool. Whip cream until it ribbons well, but is not too stiff; fold into mixture.

Freeze as in other ice-cream recipes (p.196).

When nearly set, beat with a whisk and fold in stiffly beaten egg-whites. Return to chill completely. Beat once or twice whilst this is happening.

Serve garnished with tangerine segments, and skinned and de-seeded muscat grapes, and with ladies fingers.

# Louisa Trotter's Christmas Trifle

A *good* trifle's the best thing out of England, but make it properly. It is a great advantage when a trifle is made with a fatless sponge and not heavy leftover pieces of Victoria sponge cake; a trifle is not the place to use up bits of stale cake and excellent small trifle sponges can be bought if you don't want to make your own.

## Ingredients

*Base*
Up to 1 lb. apricot purée, apricot jam, or quince jelly
2 x 7 inch fatless sponge cakes or 1 packet good quality small sponge cakes
Up to ¼ bottle medium dry sherry

*Custard*
5 eggs
1 teaspoon cornflour
1 pint milk (or half milk and half cream)
Vanilla pod
1½-2 ozs. castor sugar

*Topping*
4 ozs. glacé cherries
2 ozs. either crystallised apricots, crystallised pears, Carlsbad plums, etc.
Angelica leaves
1 pint double cream
4 ozs. blanched or toasted almonds
2 ozs. crystallised chestnuts
4 ozs. ratafia biscuits

For fresh fruit trifles, see *Variations*

## Method

First make up the custard. Bring to the boil the milk, together with the vanilla pod. Mix the sugar with the cornflour, add the eggs gradually and beat the mixture well until it is smooth. Remove the vanilla pod from the saucepan and pour the boiling milk onto the egg mixture, stirring all the time.

Rinse out the pan, leaving a film of cold water in the bottom. Return the custard to the pan and stir it with a wooden spoon over a low heat until it is thick. Plunge the bottom of the pan into a basin of cold water to remove any heat which *might* curdle the custard. Leave to cool while you prepare the base.

Split the sponge cakes in half across their middles; liberally spread them with the purée, jam or jelly, sandwich them together and cut into 1 inch fingers. Arrange these in a shallow trifle dish, some 12 inches across the top and about 3 inches deep.

Sprinkle the sponge fingers with plenty of sherry and pour the waiting custard over them. Cool the trifle base completely. (If the bowl is glass, wipe away any condensation from the sides, as this will look unsightly when the trifle is cold.)

Prepare all the topping ingredients — the actual quantities will depend on the area of trifle to be covered and this is bound to vary slightly. Put each topping ready on a separate plate.

Cut the crystallised apricots or pears and chestnuts and Carlsbad plums into attractive quarters. Cut long spikes of angelica. Empty the packet of ratafias to free them from biscuit crumbs. Make sure that the blanched or toasted almonds are cold or they will melt the cream.

Whip the cream until it just stands in peaks but doesn't look as though it will be cheese at any minute! Spread a thick layer over the trifle.

Starting on the outside edge, put a 'tight' circle of alternate cherries and ratafias round the whole perimeter of the dish. Next fill a piping bag fitted with a large 'rose' tube and make a second circle of round swirls of cream.

Then make a circle of apricot quarters, alternated with an equal swirl of thick rich cream; stick the cream with two or three blanched whole almonds. Next put a circle of cherries and ratafias.

Continue like this until you are within 6 inches of the centre, when you can introduce the more expensive things like the chestnuts, apricots or pears, Carlsbad plums or whatever, all cut into quarters. Arrange these in the centre section with the angelica spikes.

Finish the top by sticking more whole almonds into the first circle of cream swirls if you are feeling in a really luxurious mood.

An attractive and unusual centre can be made if you crystalise a huge, blowsy scented rose. This is easily done by carefully detaching the best of the petals and painting each one on both sides with a solution of gum arabic, then dredging the petals with castor sugar. You *must* ensure that the entire surface is covered or moisture will make the rose petals turn black. Dry the petals in an airing cupboard overnight. Re-form attractively in the shape of a 'blown' rose. The petals will keep for weeks in an air-tight storage jar, so can be made well in advance.

*Variations* You may prefer to make a fresh fruit trifle and in this case use fresh fruits only for decoration and stick them into the bed of whipped cream at the last moment so that the juices do not 'draw' and spoil the look of the trifle. A purée of the fruit can replace the jam in the sponge cakes. Particularly suitable fruits to use are strawberries or raspberries (wild or garden) and fresh apricots.

A nice alternative is to make an almond trifle. Roughly chop some ratafia biscuits and add these to the cake base. Cover the whipped cream (which in this case should be slightly sweetened) completely with whole blanched almonds and nothing else.

Other acceptable variations are to use Madeira, brandy or rum instead of the sherry. With fresh raspberries, use Kirsch in both the base and the whipped cream topping.

# The Bentinck Christmas Cake

## Ingredients

2½ teacupsful flour
1 teacupful cream
¾ teacupful moist
  (brown) sugar
½ lb. raisins
1 tablespoonful vinegar

½ teacupful melted butter
1 teacupful treacle
2 eggs
½ oz. powdered ginger
1 teaspoonful bicarbonate
  of soda

# Method

Make the butter sufficiently warm to melt it, but do not allow it to oil; put the flour into a basin, add to it the sugar, ginger and raisins, which should be stoned and cut into small pieces. When these dry ingredients are thoroughly mixed, stir in the butter, cream, treacle, and well-whisked eggs, and beat the mixture for a few minutes. Mix the soda with the dry ingredients, taking great care to leave no lumps, then stir the vinegar into the dough. When it is wetted, put the cake into a greased tin or mould, place it in a moderate oven immediately, and bake it from $1\frac{3}{4}$ to $2\frac{1}{4}$ hours.

*Time* $1\frac{3}{4}$ to $2\frac{1}{4}$ hours.

*Sufficient* for about $1\frac{1}{2}$ lbs. of cake.

*Note* I add a teaspoon of mixed spice together with the ginger, and also 8 ozs. chopped mixed peel.

---

# Bentinck Mincemeat

---

## Ingredients

1 lb. currants
1 lb. seedless raisins
1 lb. good suet
Grated rind and juice of
  2 lemons
$\frac{1}{4}$ pint Jamaica rum
8 ozs. chopped dried
  apricots
Level teaspoon ginger

1 lb. sultanas
8 ozs. chopped peel
4 Cox's apples, shredded
  with their skins on
Grated rind and juice of
  2 oranges
2 teaspoons mixed spice
  (less or more as your
  taste demands)

## Method

Mix all the ingredients together and fill into sterilised jars, cover and tie down. Store in a cool place.

# Yeast Cake

## Ingredients

1½ lbs. flour
¼ lb. butter
3 eggs
¾ lb. currants

½ pint milk
3 ozs. distillery (brewers) yeast
½ lb. (white moist) sugar
2 ozs. candied peel

## Method

Put the milk and butter into a saucepan, and shake it round over the fire until the butter is melted, but do not allow the milk to become very hot. Put the flour and sugar into a basin, stir it to the milk and butter, the yeast dissolved in a little cold milk, and the eggs which should be well beaten, and form the whole into a smooth dough. Let it stand in a warm place, covered with a cloth, to rise, and when sufficiently risen add the currants and candied peel cut into thin slices. When all the ingredients are thoroughly mixed, line 2 moderate-sized cake tins with greased paper, which should be put 6 inches higher than the tin; pour in the mixture, let it stand to rise again for another ½ hour, and then bake the cakes in a brisk oven for about 1½ hours. If the tops of them become too brown, cover them with paper until they are done through. A few drops of essence of lemon, or a little grated nutmeg, may be added if this flavour is liked.

*Time* 1¼ to 1½ hours

*Sufficient* to make 2 moderate-sized cakes.

This, being a Yorkshire recipe, was given to me by Johnny's cook, and she says they always eat it on Christmas Eve with butter and Wensleydale Cheese; and a glass of Madeira or port is drunk to see Christmas in.

*Note* Use half the quantity dried yeast.

# Rum or Brandy Butter

## Ingredients

4 ozs. unsalted butter

4 tablespoons Jamaica rum

1 teaspoon orange rind

4 ozs. soft brown sugar

1 tablespoon orange juice

$\frac{1}{4}$ teaspoon cinnamon

## Method

Cream together butter and sugar, gradually add the rest of the ingredients.

# Christmas Pudding

## Ingredients

To make 2 x 4 pound puddings:

$\frac{1}{2}$ lb. self-raising flour

$\frac{1}{2}$ lb. ground almonds

$\frac{3}{4}$ lb. sultanas

$\frac{3}{4}$ lb. whole glacé cherries

2 ozs. chopped angelica

4 ozs. whole sweet almonds

4 ozs. crystallised
  chestnuts

6 eggs

$\frac{1}{2}$ lb. fresh white breadcrumbs

$\frac{3}{4}$ lb. stoned raisins
  (muscatels)

4 ozs. crystallised
  apricots

1 lb. Barbados sugar

12 ozs. cold, hard, unsalted
  butter

1 pint sweet brown ale such          Juice and rind of 1 lemon
  as barley wine                              and 1 orange
      6 tablespoons Benedictine (2 miniature bottles)

## Method

Grate the butter. Beat the eggs. Grate the orange and lemon rind and squeeze the juice and add to the beer and Benedictine. Combine all the dry ingredients. Mix well with the liquids. Put into buttered basins, cover with foil and steam for 5 hours for the first steaming, and then a further 3 hours on the day of eating.

# Frosted Fruits

Beat up 2 egg-whites until foaming but not stiff.

With a clean brush 'paint' each piece of fruit (dip smaller fruits like grapes) all over. Dredge well with castor or granulated sugar: leave to dry before arranging attractively, using wooden sticks (cocktail) to help hold the pieces where you would have them.

# Stuffed Dates

Make up almond paste (p.175). Pit some fresh dates, press a knob of paste into the cavity. Dredge with castor sugar. Top with a split almond, glacé cherry, angelica or crystallised pineapple.

Store in airtight tin.

The paste can be flavoured with sherry, rum, Cointreau etc. Prunes, dried apricots, if of good quality, can be done in this way.

# Louisa Trotter's Christmas Punch

## Ingredients

3 lemons: juice and rind
4 ozs. castor sugar
½ bottle dry gin

Bottle dry white wine
1 doz. coriander seeds
¼ bottle white rum
½ pint water

## Method

Pare the lemons, squeeze the juice; put into an enamel or stainless steel pan with the sugar, coriander seeds and water. Slowly bring to the boil and simmer for 5 minutes. Strain, wash out the pan and return this syrup to the pan. Add all the other ingredients and bring to boiling point, but do not permit to boil.

Serve immediately in *small* quantities; the reaction is sure, and caution is advised!

# Isabella Beeton's Bacchus Cup

## Ingredients

½ bottle dry Champagne
½ bottle dry sherry
⅛ pint brandy
Liqueur glass Noyau

1 tablespoon castor sugar
Bottle of seltzer
   (or soda) water
Ice

## Method

Put the Champagne, sherry, brandy, Noyau and sugar into a glass jug. Let it stand for an hour. Add ice, soda water, and serve at once.

# Gemma Jones' 'Kalte Ente'

As Louisa Trotter was a friend of the Kaiser, I thought it a good idea to ask Vere Norgrove of London's famous Walton's Restaurant to 'bend' this traditional German cold punch for present-day use. Here is what he came up with.

*Kalte Ente* (Cold Duck) is a form of fruit cup based on *Sekt* (German Sparkling wine), such as Schloss Saarfels, plus twice the quantity of a dry Moselle or Rhine wine, or even a German red wine poured on to sugared slices of fresh lemon, and served chilled.

The amount of Sekt can be increased or decreased (in the case of the latter, soda water should be added), and there are numerous further variants such as the addition of other fresh fruits (notably peaches) or a glass of liqueur such as Crème de Cassis (which is what you'll get if you go to Walton's restaurant) or Curaçao, depending on one's whim.

# Mary Phillips' Brandy Toddy

## Ingredients

Bottle red wine
  (Burgundy type)
½ bottle brandy

2 cinnamon sticks
Finely-pared rind of one
  orange

2 ozs. castor sugar

## Method

Carefully remove the rind from the orange with a potato peeler. Bring this to the boil, together with the cinnamon, sugar and red wine. Do not permit the liqueur actually to boil. Pour in the brandy: re-heat, allowing the toddy to ignite if it will.

Serve this in modest portions as the effects are strange but good!

# Index of Recipes